BETTER RÉSUMÉS FOR COMPUTER PERSONNEL

by
Adele Lewis
Former President and Founder
Career Blazers Agency, Inc.

and

Berl Hartman
Director, Database Products Development
Computer Corporation of America

BARRON'S

BARRON'S EDUCATIONAL SERIES, INC.
New York • London • Toronto • Sydney

All inquiries should be addressed to:
Barron's Educational Series, Inc.
250 Wireless Boulevard
Hauppauge, New York 11788

Library of Congress Catalog Card No. 84-184749

International Standard Book No. 0-8120-2860-0

Library of Congress Cataloging in Publication Data

PRINTED IN THE UNITED STATES OF AMERICA

789   100   987654.

Contents

Introduction

If you are reading these words in a bookstore or library, trying to decide whether this book is worth your time and money, let us help you telescope the decision-making process.

We assume that, having turned to this page, you are either an executive or a professional with an interest in improving or changing your career. We assume you know that a powerful, effective résumé is one essential tool toward accomplishing your goal.

We assume also that you want to continue working in your current career area; or you are changing career fields but know precisely in what new area you want to apply past career interests, skills, and accomplishments. (If you are less than sure of your next career move, you will find valuable tips in Chapter 5. You may want to read that chapter first and conduct further research on your own before using the rest of the book.)

From these assumptions we frame our entire universe of prospective readers, and we welcome you among them. Good luck in your new or improved career.

The Art of Job Hunting

Open the pages of any newspaper to the Help Wanted section and what do you find? Page after page of jobs in the computer industry with titles such as "Systems Analyst," "Q.A. Testing Specialist," "UNIX Workstation Project Leader," "Customer Support Specialist," "CICS Programmer." These are the jobs that will need to be filled in the coming months and years as the Computer Revolution continues. You may already have the training and experience that qualifies you for one of these jobs; or perhaps you're a recent college graduate with a few computer-related courses to your credit; or you may even be someone in an entirely unrelated job who would like to break into this booming new field.

Regardless of your background, education, or previous experience, chances are you do not enjoy the process of looking for a job.

We once did a survey to discover responses to the question "How do you view the job hunting experience?" Answers ranged from "I dread it," and "Definitely NOT my favorite pastime," to "One of the most stressful experiences I have lived through," "An unpleasant ordeal," and "It's harder than working." Occasionally—very occasionally—we received a positive reply. Some individuals reported that they found it a positive, challenging activity.

Why do most people, even those in the computer industry where there is no shortage of well-paid, interesting jobs, actually dread job hunting? Why do only a few (less than 5 percent) actually enjoy it? We've come to the conclusion that looking for and getting a job is a skill; for those very few people who intuitively know how to use that skill, job hunting is an exciting, rewarding experience. Conversely, for those not possessing this skill, job hunting can be a depressing, unpleasant task. Fortunately, this skill can be easily learned. Once acquired, it will stay with you for the rest of your life. But like any other skill, it requires some thought, careful analysis, and huge amounts of self-discipline, determination, and perseverance before it can be executed successfully. Once you are armed with the proper tools for job hunting, finding your "place in the sun" can be a dynamic as well as rewarding process.

In looking for a job you should always **aim** for the best available, and try to avoid settling for less.

Why not go for the "Lead Programmer" position, instead of settling for simple "COBOL Programmer"? Or move into a job where you'll learn a new technology, language, or database? The more you stretch yourself, the more interesting the work, and the more valuable you become to your employer.

But you must maintain an open and realistic attitude, evaluating each opportunity with a flexible and farsighted point of view. You may have to give up temporarily some management responsibility or even take a cut in pay to find a more technically challenging job where you will learn something new that ultimately will be of more value to you.

Try very hard not to be **rigid.** Be open to new ideas, give a great deal of thought to the possibility of relocation, carefully consider your long-term goals as well as what is expedient for the moment. While we believe in trying to hold out for the very best, we are also aware that a job is often what you make it. Even if, at the onset, you don't find the perfect job, the one you get may be a very important step in your climb to success. We've seen Administrative Assistants become Software Engineers, Key Punch Operators turn into Application Programmers, and Dictionary Data Entry Clerks move up to become Database Administrators.

The Skill (or Art) of Job Hunting/Successful Career Strategy

You must know exactly what **kind** of job you want and be sure you have the appropriate qualifications. We cannot emphasize this too strongly. We've had to turn down otherwise qualified applicants because they couldn't answer the question "What kind of job are you looking for?"

You must apply for the right job no matter how high your IQ, how perfect your job search is conducted, how superior your references. If you want to be a Systems Analyst and don't have the qualifications for that position, you're heading for failure. That's Step One. *Be sure you are qualified (both in appropriate education and work history) for the position you are seeking.*

Now that you know what kind of job you're looking for, you have to let the world know you are ready, willing, and available. That's Step Two toward mastering the skill of job hunting. The best possible vehicle for this information is your *résumé.* Obviously, it must be smashing. It must look good, read well, and—more than anything else—generate enough interest in you to get you invited to an interview. Chapter 2 will show you, in a logical, step-by-step manner, exactly how this is done.

Step Three follows: What you should do with your résumé—how you choose targeted employers or employment agencies (known as Head Hunters) and how you write covering letters that will synergistically maximize the impact of your résumé. This will be thoroughly discussed in Chapters 5 and 6.

We will also discuss job sources tailored to the computer industry. A successful career strategist must know which are the superior agencies, professional groups, and trade journals that will be the most useful.

You may not yet know a computer from a refrigerator, but you still may have valuable skills that can be put to work in the computer industry.

Chapter 7 will outline the skill of interviewing, perhaps the very heart of job getting. We will discuss the probability of a series of interviews and how to handle them. We'll show you how to convert that job interview into a job offer.

We are convinced that learning and using these job-hunting skills will create positive results, and no more will you view job hunting in only negative terms. You will find that **you** control your job search, and it will lift you to a new level of self-confidence.

Contents and Style of a Résumé

Transcribing your skills, education, work experience, goals, and ambitions onto a sheet of paper or two may be the most difficult, as well as most important, task facing you in your job search. Is it actually possible to encapsulate your three-dimensional self, your experience, your abilities, your uniqueness, on a two-dimensional piece of 8½ by 11-inch paper?

Granted that the paper cannot possibly reveal all the many aspects that compose the total you, then what is its purpose? In this complex world—where distance, time, and sheer number of individuals mitigate against personal involvements between employers and employees—the résumé has been adopted as an embodiment of you. Because it must represent you when you cannot speak for yourself, it has become a very important job-hunting document.

Think of your résumé as your agent, your representative, your mini-business or professional dossier, your emissary, your single most important self-advertisement. It's your go-between. In other words, the résumé represents you! It is your statement of self, to be distributed among colleagues, to be sent in answer to advertisements, to be mailed to targeted employers. You send it for their review and, ultimately, to generate interviews.

Even though computer-related jobs are appearing in every segment of the economy, the competition can still be fierce. For every job opening we have, we may review one hundred résumés. Your résumé needs to distinguish you from the rest and show that **you** can do the job better than anyone else. Employers tell us they spend only ten or twenty seconds scanning a résumé before they decide to read it word for word. In other words, you have no more than ten or twenty seconds to impress the employer enough to actually read your résumé. If your résumé doesn't pass the test of a twenty-second scan, it is simply discarded.

Your résumé must immediately show that you know where you are going with your career and have just the right background at your current level to qualify you for the position in question. But let's begin at the top.

Every résumé must identify and describe the writer. It **must** include:

- ☐ Your name, address, and telephone number
- ☐ A description of your educational history
- ☐ Hardware and software you have worked with
- ☐ A description of your work history
- ☐ Work-related honors or citations

☐ Security clearance, if any
☐ Publications, if any

It **may** also include:

☐ Your job objective or career goal
☐ Computer-related courses you have taken
☐ A capsule description of your work history
☐ Memberships in any professional organizations
☐ Foreign languages you may know
☐ Information on hobbies, especially if they relate in some way or show diversity of interests
☐ Military service, if any
☐ Willingness to travel or relocate
☐ Personal data—marital status, children

It should **not** include the following information:

☐ Reasons for leaving past jobs
☐ Past salaries or present salary requirements
☐ Personal data—age, height, weight
☐ Names of spouse or children
☐ A photograph of yourself
☐ Names and addresses of references

Résumé Styles

Although every résumé should contain a brief, concise summary of your work history and educational background, the style or approach differs in the arrangement of this data. Though there are several résumé styles we believe the chronological is the most effective, and we strongly recommend that you choose this approach in writing your résumé. We will, however, discuss others as well and evaluate each style.

Despite minor variations, there are basically four different résumé styles or approaches.

☐ Chronological (Historical)
☐ Functional
☐ Synoptic/Amplified
☐ Imaginative, Creative, or Informal

We'll discuss each, with consideration of their usefulness.

The Chronological (Historical) Résumé

As the name implies, this style presents the information in chronological sequence. The succession of facts must be presented in **reverse** chronological order, starting with the present or most recent experience and moving backward in time.

As with any résumé, start with your name, address, and phone number. It is almost traditional in the computer industry to list your education first. There are no hard and fast rules about this, and certainly if you have a good, solid background of experience but have not completed your degree, then it makes sense to place the education at the end of the résumé instead. Usually, however, your most advanced degree is shown first, followed in reverse order by all other degrees. Again dates should always be used. State the name of the university, city, state, degree earned, and the dates attended. Academic honors would be included in this grouping.

If you have opted to use a career objective or résumé capsule, place it near the top of the first page. Also include a list of the hardware and software that you have worked with. The listing should detail the major machines, operating systems, languages, database systems, and software packages with which you feel truly comfortable.

Your work history should list each job (in reverse chronological order), specifying your job title, the name of your employer, the address (city and state; number and name of street are not necessary) and a summary of your duties and responsibilities. These summaries should be brief but specific. Always include dates; they can be in vertical columns to the left of the other information, on a line before the description of each job held, or included as an integral part of the paragraph. Generally, placing the dates in a vertical column is perferable, as employers like to be able to determine at a glance the times involved.

The chronological résumé should be brief and take no more than two pages. This type of résumé offers a clear, concise picture of you, and it is probably the easiest to assimilate in a quick reading. Without exception, the chronological format was preferred by the corporate executives we've talked to; they felt it does the best job of indicating an individual's direction, background, accomplishments, and general qualifications.

The Functional Résumé

As its name implies, the functional résumé emphasizes the writer's qualifications and abilities. This approach rejects a chronological sequence of employment and educational history, and instead provides analyses of particular professional strengths. The employment strengths or skills are the important facts in this style of résumé.

Your work history, volunteer experience, and educational record are fragmented into significant talents, and each skill is listed separately. Because these functions or responsibilities usually have crossed over a number of jobs, the sequence of job history has been sacrificed to emphasize ability. Names of employers and dates are omitted from this section of the résumé, since the expertise has been gained from more than one position.

The functional résumé should be brief, concise, and well structured. It should start with your name, address, and phone number, your job objective, and a résumé summary (if needed). The body of the résumé should consist of four or five paragraphs, each one heading a particular area of expertise or involvement.

The skills paragraphs should be listed in order of importance. We define the most important skill as the function that is most similar to your present career goal or job objective.

Typical headings might be Applications Programming, Systems Analysis, Project Management, Database Support, and so on. A brief summary of your accomplishments in each category would follow.

Though this type of résumé has gained in popularity over the past few years, very few employers, personnel men and women, and staff managers approve of this approach. Our employment experts tell us that they become very suspicious of the functional résumé. They feel it is often used to cover up a spotty work record (for example, seven jobs in four years or a long period of unemployment), to exaggerate certain abilities, or to disguise some "whole truth." One corporate executive put it succinctly when he said, "It raises more questions than it answers."

The only situation that lends itself to the functional résumé is when you are attempting a career change. In that case, this style résumé may be advantageous because it shows in a glance the kinds of jobs within your capacity. If you are trying to parlay your experience in an unrelated field and show its relevancy to the computer industry, you might use the functional résumé with a certain modification. Because most résumé readers feel that résumés lose their effectiveness if dates or names of employers are not shown, you should overcome this by adding a very concise historical (always in reverse chronological order) listing of employers, job titles, and job descriptions with the appropriate dates. This history should follow your description by function.

The Synoptic/Amplified Résumé

The synoptic/amplified résumé is weak because, by definition, it requires the use of two or more pages and hence important information can be easily overlooked. The word *synoptic* means "affording a general view of a whole" while to *amplify* is to expand (as in statement) by the use of detail or illustration or by closer analysis. As the name suggests, this résumé gives both a general overview or simplification of your background as well as an expansive, detailed description.

The first page consists of all pertinent data such as name,

address, and telephone number, plus résumé capsule, hardware and software listings, job objective (if included), employment history (with job titles and names and addresses of employers) and dates of employment. Educational background is also included on the first page, and the entire history is arranged in reverse chronological order.

The succeeding pages repeat the employment history, but the job record is expanded or "amplified" to include a short narration describing the duties or responsibilities for each position held. This résumé is most effective if the duties and responsibilities encompass more than the job title implies, or if the work experience has been a long and varied one.

Although we see this style of résumé often, we do not recommend its use. The main disadvantage is that it may run on for several pages, taxing the reader's patience and taking too much of his time. Our corporate résumé readers tell us this style implies a certain arrogance and feeling of self-importance. With any résumé of more than two pages you take a chance on missing a thorough read-through, and with each additional page there also comes the increasing possibility of loss of a page, in effect, nullifying the impact of your résumé.

The Imaginative/Creative Résumé

You may feel that an imaginative, highly unusual approach is the ideal thing to shake loose your résumé from the pack. Using artwork, illustrations, cartoons, or a unique format may very well create an impression, but not necessarily a good one.

We have received résumés that were over two feet long, wound up like a scroll; very, very small ones put together to resemble a passport (the print so reduced you would have to use a magnifying glass, if you wanted to read it); résumés in the format of menus, play bills, calendars, stock certificates, and even a summons. True, these résumés caught the eye. They amused and charmed us, but they did not sustain enough interest to become effective. Such résumés are usually difficult to read, unprofessional, and impossible to file. Corporate employers share our opinion that a résumé is a business matter and, accordingly, should be presented in a businesslike, professional manner.

Putting Yourself on Paper   **3**

When preparing your résumé, always keep in mind the purpose of that résumé—to serve as a personal advertisement, generating enough interest in you to secure an interview. As an effective advertisement, it should be attractive, easy to read, concise, and informative. Because the chronological résumé is the most preferred style, we will use this approach in showing you how to write your résumé.

The information contained in the résumé should be presented in the following order (the optional items are shown in parenthesis):

- ☐ Identifying information
- ☐ (Summary or résumé capsule)
- ☐ Educational history
- ☐ (Career or job objective)
- ☐ Hardware/software information
- ☐ Employment history
- ☐ Honors or citations, if any
- ☐ Security clearance, if any
- ☐ Publications, if any
- ☐ Membership in professional organizations

Including mention of military service, knowledge of foreign languages, hobbies, a willingness to travel or relocate, and other personal information is optional, and there is no prescribed order. However, this information should appear near the end of the résumé.

In deciding whether to include a job objective and/or a job summary, consider that your present or most recent job description should be on the first page. If your objective and/or summary are too long, it may be better to shorten both or omit one of them.

Identifying Information

Always start with your identifying material in a conspicuous position, either flush left (leaving room for the margin) or on the top center (again leave about ¾ to 1½ inches for the margin). Give your complete name, street address, city, state, zip code and phone number, complete with area code. If you can be reached at the office, that number should also be listed.

The use of the summary, also called a résumé capsule, is optional, and sometimes can be combined with the hardware/ software listing. To be effective, it must include information indicating that you are indeed qualified for the position sought. Although optional, we have been told by more than one personnel director of an important computer company that this is the first piece of information they scan. The beauty of the summary is that it gives you the power of the functional résumé and, at the same time, excludes all of its disadvantages. Here is your opportunity to combine and build on similar aspects of your background which may have been acquired over a period of many years in a number of different positions.

Suppose one of your biggest accomplishments occurred in an early job. If you were using a straight reverse-chronological style presentation, this important information might not be noticed by the reader. It probably would appear near the bottom of the page or possibly on the second page, and would very likely be missed. The summary allows you to emphasize it at the beginning. It is the space where you can list the highlights or whatever else you might consider your biggest career accomplishment, regardless of when that was.

The summary should consist of one **strong** sentence, three or four at the most. Those sentences should be enough to highlight the aspects of your background that will most appeal to a potential employer.

Here are some samples of summary paragraphs:

> "B.S. in Computer Science, combined with over 4 years experience in programming and analysis, including extensive coding at the assembler level for operating systems and telecommunications."

> "MBA degree plus 7 years of diversified experience in the analysis, design, and implementation of financial and material management systems. Trained in a variety of on-line systems, including CICS, IMS/DL1 and DMS."

> "From helicopter technician to computer operator via 2-year training course at GE Institute. Fully versed in MVS, VS1, and JES operator procedures and commands."

> "Complete responsibility for verification of input and output from highly complex payroll systems. JCL Modifications and parameter substitutions to adjust to changing system requirements."

We suggest that you write down every skill, responsibility, job duty, and accomplishment that will qualify you for your next position. Think of every problem you had some part in solving, any new idea you contributed to which was ultimately used by your employer, any achievements or capabilities you have which would demonstrate or suggest that you can do the job better than anyone else.

Study your list, and pare it down to five or six points. Combine those that are similar in function so that you can write a brief narrative that has a convincing tone to it. Be brief. Choose your words carefully.

We've been told by recruiters that if the summary sustains their interest, they will continue and read the résumé in its entirety. You may have to write several drafts—shortening sentences, changing a word here and there, deleting unnecessary adjectives or phrases that might be repetitive. Work on it until you have it perfect.

The summary or capsule résumé is the best way of emphasizing solid work background and of highlighting specific qualifications to a targeted employer. While it often involves retyping the résumé for each potential employer, the capsule résumé can be the only part of your résumé that does have to be adjusted to suit different employer's needs.

Educational History

Start with your most advanced degree and include the name and location of the college or university you attended, the degrees you earned, and the year you graduated. Mention your major field of study and all career-oriented scholarships and academic awards. Thereafter, list—in reverse chronological order—all other degrees until you reach your B.A. or B.S. Include the same information for each as described for the advanced degree. Though abbreviations generally should not be used in résumés, it is acceptable and correct in listing your degrees; for example, Ph.D., M.S., B.A., B.S. If you have attended college, it is not necessary to include information concerning high school.

A recent graduate should mention his or her grade point average if it is 3.5 or higher. Obviously, there is no point in calling attention to a C average. If you were Phi Beta Kappa, Summa, or Magna Cum Laude, or if you received other high academic honors, no matter what level of experience you have, by all means mention it.

Computer Courses

Your level of experience in the computer field will determine whether or not you should include the names of specific computer courses you have taken. For example, if you are a recent graduate or are changing careers, it is a good idea to name any computer science or technical courses you have successfully completed, either in college or at a technical institute. On the other hand, a computer science major need not indicate every course by name, but simply mention the area of concentration or special interest.

Classes or seminars you may have attended can also be included, especially those offered by vendors such as IBM, DEC, or other hardware and software houses.

As your real-world experience and expertise grow, much educational information becomes less relevant. The one exception may be certain prestigious seminars which, by your very attendance, indicate a high level of expertise.

Hardware and Software

Anyone looking for a job involving programming, software development, or operations should consider this section an absolute requirement. It is also highly recommended for other jobs such as Database Administration, Systems Analyst, Quality Assurance, and Data Communications. It is less important for administrators, general analysts, trainers, documentation specialists, or researchers. However, it is **not** recommended for sales positions, since it gives the résumé a technical flavor which is not appropriate. If your job falls into one of the categories for which this section is recommended, it is probably the most important part of your résumé, and therefore it should be placed in a very prominent position, preferably on the upper third of the page. If this section is not included, it is much more difficult for the reader to obtain this vital information.

The hardware/software section should include the following:

☐ Hardware and software (together, to save space)
☐ Machines (by category and manufacturer)
☐ Operating systems
☐ Languages (those in which you are truly fluent)
☐ Database systems (if you've worked with them or are very familiar with them)
☐ Other software packages: statistical, librarians, report writers, text editors, graphics, performance monitors
☐ TP access methods and/or monitors

If your knowledge of a particular language or package is limited, you should state this, either in parentheses or by following the list with a separate line titled "Familiar with." This section of the résumé will obviously be discussed in your interview, and if you've made any claims which are questionable, you will lessen your credibility and everything else on your résumé will be suspect. Here, as in the entire job-hunting process, it is imperative to be honest. Employers are likely to hire someone and then train them on a particular system, machine, or language if the résumé qualifies in other respects. You don't need to list every single machine, especially if you've worked on a great many. It is probably better to use categories such as: IBM 370, 43XX, 30XX. Putting very old or very out-of-date hardware or software down can also give the impression of your not only being dated but also of padding your résumé.

Here are some typical samples of the hardware/software sections:

"IBM 303X, 4341, 3705, 8100, OS/MVS, VS1, VS2, DOS, VM/CMS, TSO, ROSCOE, CICS, IMS, DL/1, DMS, DTMS, ADABAS, TOTAL, DATAMANAGER, COBOL, BAL, NCP, ACF, SNA, SDLC, X.25"

"FORTRAN, COBOL, PLI, ALGOL, APL, UNIX, C, BASIC; Assembly languages for the PDP-8, PDP-9/15, PDP-11, GE 635/645, H-316/516/716, NOVA 1200, XDS 9300, SIGMA 5/7, DDP 24, IBM 1620, IBM 1130/1800; *some experience* with H-60/6000, H-60/6, IBM 360/370, CDC 6600/7600; IBM 4300, VM/CMS, DEC/20, VAX, PRIME, IBM P.C., TI 994; experience with analog and hybrid systems"

IBM 370/148, 158, Amdahl 470/V5, XEROX 9700; ADABAS, COMPLETE, Natural, Model 204 (User Language only), STAIRS; COBOL, Assembler, (limited PL/1); OS/VS1, OS/VS2 (MVS), Utilities, JCL, Service Aids, etc.; TSO, Wylbur, MITS, PANVALET, Librarian"

Sometimes the hardware/software section is separated into separate areas; for example:

HARDWARE:	IBM 370/168 3033 4341-II, Prime Series 50, HP-3000
SOFTWARE:	IBM OS/VS2 (MVS), JCL, CLIST, EXEC, IMS, TSO/SPF, VM/CMS, PANVALET, IMAGE, QUERY, PRIMOS, DBMS
LANGUAGE:	COBOL, MIMS

Clearance

If you have applied for and received government clearance for work in government or the defense industry, it should be included together with the dates, level, and governmental agency which granted it. For example:

"Secret Security Clearance while serving in the U.S. Army from July 1975 to November 1979"

Obviously if you don't have any clearance, either because you have never applied or because you have applied and been turned down, then omit this section completely.

As with the summary, the job objective or career goal is strictly optional. The career goal or job objective provides the tone, direction, and major emphasis of the complete document. Every succeeding word will be read in reference to those two or three sentences of the job objective, should you choose to include this feature.

We've seen excellent results with résumés that include objectives as well as those that omit this information. The purpose of the objective is to describe succinctly the position you want by job title, function, and/or industry.

The job objective must logically connect with the balance of your résumé. You should avoid stating objectives that are too confining; you don't want one that will cancel out opportunities that might be of interest to you. On the other hand, be careful of clichés ("a challenging position which offers an opportunity to grow") or overly vague generalities ("a position that is both rewarding and stimulating"). Such statements are meaningless, and the reader might infer that you are unsure of what you want.

If there is a specific job title that precisely defines your goals, by all means use it. For example:

☐ Programmer
☐ Systems Analyst
☐ Manager Product Support
☐ Senior Programmer/Analyst
☐ Database Designer

These titles have a certain crisp simplicity about them and demonstrate clearly what direction you're heading for.

In deciding whether or not to include the job objective, consider also that omitting this objective lets the prospective employer determine if your qualifications are appropriate for a job you may not have considered. On the other hand, the advantage of using a well-stated objective is that it can target your résumé to the appropriate manager or section head within a company.

One particular situation in which you may want to use it is if you are seeking a management position and have made up your mind to settle for nothing less. Clearly state that in the objective. For example:

> "A challenging management position in the Application Development area"

If you are not clearly headed down the management track, however, it is better not to rule out a role as an individual contributor by such a strong statement. Some examples of more general objectives are:

> "Sales position with a quality company dealing in systems software for the IBM Mainframe Market"

"A position in Software Technical Support or Systems Programming".

"Technical writer of end user documentation"

"Technical staff position developing, maintaining, or converting on-line database systems

Though we have repeatedly said that the use of a career goal is optional, there is one very definite situation when a job objective **must** be used: When you are trying to redirect your career.

In this unpredictable economy, where little is certain and industries are constantly evolving or dissolving, it is not suprising that many individuals change careers several times in their working lifetime. Perhaps you are in a field in which you feel your career is going nowhere, or maybe you're in an area where there is a dearth of jobs and a plethora of candidates. You might have been phased out, laid off, underemployed, misemployed, or just plain unemployed. Whatever the reason, you may believe that the answer to your employment problems lies in the computer industry.

Certainly, this is an industry which has undergone unprecedented growth in the last ten years. It's a field where the supply of trained personnel has not kept up with the demand, a field where, as computers have become more and more pervasive throughout society, there have been openings for people with a wide variety of skills and talents. For instance, if your background is in teaching science to high school students and you want to change to a career as a technical instructor, simply state your new goal and back it up by summarizing your employment history. For example:

"An opportunity to parlay eight years teaching experience as a high school teacher to a position as a technical instructor in the computer industry"

Or suppose you are a housewife returning to the job market, a former math major who's done a great deal of volunteer work in the community. Your job objective might read:

"An opportunity to combine my mathematical problem-solving ability with my organizational and interpersonal skills in a computer/service related job"

Another example might be to turn your experience as a freelance author into a job as a technical writer:

"A position as a technical writer which will take advantage of my 5 years experience as a freelance feature writer"

In these instances, state your career goal, **followed** by the same information you would have included in a résumé written for your original field.

The heart of your résumé is the section that describes your experience or employment history. It is important to remember that your résumé must be honest as well as logical. Never put anything in your résumé that is not 100 percent true. Stay with the truth, even if you feel a small exaggeration or distortion might make you more marketable. Any information that is not true can become an insurmountable liability. Employers usually expect that a new employee will require some training, and they are quite willing to do so. If, however, you claimed certain strengths and are unable to demonstrate those abilities, you can be sure your credibility on all other matters will be questioned.

Begin your employment history with your present or most recent experience. Work backwards, treating each position as an independent entry. Each job mentioned should include the name and address (city and state; no streets or numbers) of the employer, the dates involved (month and year), and a concise description of your responsibilities. If you are presently employed, use the present tense in describing your current position and, obviously, the past tense for former jobs. Use only implied pronouns in crisp, simple language. Writing in the third person (he/she) is stylistically objectionable, as well as suggesting a certain detachment. Using the first person (I) is redundant; plainly the person reading the résumé is aware that you are the subject of your own résumé. For example, compare the following "bits" of information:

"She/he was responsible for all system support of CICS"

"I was responsible for all system support of CICS"

"Responsible for all system support of CICS"

Always give the name of each company you have worked for, including your present employer, even though you may wish this to be considered confidential. You will weaken your résumé by not including specific names. Once we received a résumé without any company identifying information, and decided we were not interested in that candidate. Luckily, he followed up with a phone call. It was only when he told us the name of the company, which happened to be a direct competitor, that we realized his experience was exactly what we were looking for. It is understandable that you might be circumspect about the fact that you are looking for a job. However, all agencies and employers treat this information as confidential.

Your goal in this section of the résumé is to make as much as you can of each position you have had, while keeping the descriptions as brief as possible. Describe your major responsibilities while concentrating heavily on the accomplishments you can legitimately own or share.

Always be as specific as possible and avoid generalities or long descriptions of the company or department you worked for. Describe exactly what you did and what your responsibilities were. If you mention a system, outline your role. Did you design it, code it, test it, or maintain it? Did you "participate in" or were you entirely "responsible for"? Mention the names of all relevant software, including language and type of on-line system or editor if applicable.

Think of as many problems as you can that faced you and you were able to solve. Our questionnaire on page 23 will help you to organize these thoughts. Mention any improvements you were responsible for, any ideas adopted by your employer. Describe actions you took to solve problems and the positive conditions that were the consequences of your efforts. Don't be shy; never be humble. But never be arrogant, either. Be proud of your achievements.

The job descriptions should be just that and, although it is important to list accomplishments, it also has to paint an accurate picture of what your daily routine included. For example, an entry such as "Increased stability of products, shortened maintenance cycle" may be fine, but the recruiter also needs to know what the product was, what your role was in it, and how you made these improvements. You might have stated that as follows:

> "As manager of product support for Environ II, introduced quality control procedures to increase stability of product and shorten maintenance cycle."

You may assume that an interviewer's interest will be piqued by each of your employment history entries, and you will be asked to elaborate on them in the interview. View each bit of information you provide as the basis of a future leading question. It's a good idea to mentally rehearse your responses as you write your job description.

Use active verbs; they give a certain power to your résumé. And choose your words carefully; make each word count. Avoid being flowery; too many adjectives, especially an overabundance of superlatives, lessens the impact of your résumé.

Keep in mind, always, that you're aiming for a 2-page résumé. Be brief, concise. Keep narratives describing each position succinct—no more than five to ten lines. Each accomplishment should be broken up into bite-sized entities for the reader to spot and digest quickly. Information concerning past positions should **not** be as long as current or recent ones. Avoid repetition—if your job responsibilities were similar in more than one job, describe in detail only the most recent position. Also, it is not necessary to use complete sentences. Indent and use "banner" statements to emphasize accomplishments. Start such entries with an asterisk (*) or dot (·) so they appear to "pop" out.

Rewrite your first draft. It may be necessary to rewrite it several times, striking out unnecessary words and phrases and tightening sentences until they say exactly what you mean.

Reread it several times, checking for spelling and grammatical errors. After several rereadings, have a friend or colleague scan it. Another person may pick up errors that you have missed and possibly suggest some additional qualifications.

Professional Societies and Publications

List all professional associations and organizations that are career related. Your membership in such groups implies dedication to your field and an ability to get along with others. If you are or have ever been an officer in any organization, be sure to mention that fact. For example:

> "Member ACM and IEEE Computer Society. Organized IEEE Seminar Series on Pascal, UNIX, and Ada."

List titles of all published articles and books you have written and note where and when they appeared. For example:

> "The New IBM Personal Computer," *ACM Newsletter*, January 1983.

> "Some Thoughts on an Ada Compiler," *Electronic News*, March 1983.

Personal Information

The items that are *very* optional are height, weight, marital status, and number of children; these may be included but they are not necessary. Age, sex, color, picture of yourself, names of spouses and children—**never** include these! Your state of health (it's always "excellent" anyway) is superfluous. If, however, you have a disability and feel you want the potential employer to know about it before the interview, mention it in your covering letter, not in the résumé. Your résumé should emphasize your **abilities**, not your disabilities. You're probably aware of the increased opportunities for people with handicaps and, in many cases, employers are actively searching for people with such problems. If this is your situation, you might be best mentioning that in your letter.

Should you include hobbies and leisure-time activities? Only if you feel a description of your avocations will enhance your image as a qualified candidate. We once came across a résumé of someone with only one year's experience. In the personal information section, he mentioned that he was a nationally ranked runner. We felt this gave an indication of the candidate's determination and "spunk," and so we decided to gamble on him, even though we didn't normally hire people at this junior level.

Any career related hobbies, of course, should be included, but remember that every word in your résumé should be there for a reason. A long list of unrelated hobbies might give the impression that all your time and energy is spent on leisure-time activities or that you are unable to sustain an interest in one or two and need dozens to stave off boredom. An individual over fifty (though age is not given, the employment and education dates give clues) participating in outdoor sports **should** include such information. A fifty-six-year-old person who is a sailing, golf, or skiing enthusiast will be visualized as a vibrant, energetic person.

Military Service

If your military service has no revelance to your career goals, simply state that you completed it and provide the date you were honorably discharged. Including such information avoids the appearance of a time lapse in your history. On the other hand, if you received special technical training and that expertise has added to your qualifications, both of those facts should be mentioned, as well as the branch of the service. Be sure to include the dates involved and give the highest rank you achieved.

References

Never, never supply the names of your references on your résumé. Not only is it unprofessional, but it can cause a lot of bother to those individuals listed. Simply state, as the last entry on your résumé, "References on Request" or "References will be furnished upon request."

Always get permission from those individuals you wish to use as references. Don't put yourself or them in the position in which any calls about you will come as a surprise to them. Try, if possible, to get references that can be reached quickly. For that reason, it is preferable to list persons who can be reached by phone rather than by mail. Make certain you have all of their current addresses and phone numbers. If you are giving a person's business phone, check to see if he or she is still employed by the same company.

If your name has been changed through marriage or for any other reason during your work or educational history, be sure that your references know you by your new name. It is wise for women who have married and have adopted their husband's name to indicate their maiden name as well. Lastly, you should only give permission to call your references when an employer has indicated that you are under serious consideration.

Photographs

Never! Never, unless you are looking for a job as a model/computer "what ever"! Not only are photographs on résumés unprofessional, but their legality is questionable. If an employer kept résumés containing photographs on file, that action could be considered a covert form of racial, sex, or age screening and, as such, could be considered illegal. But more important to you, don't prejudice your chances by sending a photo.

Reasons For Leaving Past Jobs

An emphatic NO! Your résumé should be a businesslike summary of your talents, qualifications, goals, work history, and education. Since the reasons you left previous employers do not add to that summary, they should not be included in your résumé. These reasons for leaving earlier jobs will be discussed in the interview.

Salaries, Past and Present

Salaries—neither your present minimum nor your past earnings—should be discussed or listed in your résumé. A potential employer will probably arrange a series of interviews, and the subject of salary will most often be discussed close to or at the final meeting.

Every employer we've had contact with considers salary a most confidential matter. It is considered extremely unprofessional as well as indiscreet for employees to discuss salaries among themselves. Your résumé will be seen by many individuals in the company who normally would not and **should not** know your salary range, so no indication of it should appear in your résumé.

Should you at least include your salary requirement? No. Including your salary requirements might eliminate you from certain positions in which the remuneration has not yet been decided; or it might preclude you from obtaining a certain position with an already-established higher salary. As we've indicated before, reserve your discussion of salary for the final interview.

Résumé Appearance

Visualize an employer who, after placing an ad, receives over two hundred résumés. He or she is also developing new systems, planning programs, and has a desk filled with other projects demanding attention. He or she is now faced with selecting the résumés to read more closely. Obviously, the first step is to scan. As we've mentioned earlier, our inquiries have shown that an average recruiter rarely gives more than 10 seconds attention to a résumé in deciding whether it merits a complete reading.

Put yourself in the reader's position. Do you actually read every word in every newspaper or magazine you look at? We're sure your answer is in the negative. In this fast-paced world, who has the time or even the interest? Rather, you automatically scan the material to decide which articles, advertisements, or stories are worth your time for a thorough read-through. The print media has proved that "eye appeal" is as important as content; people simply discard that which is difficult to read. And we are aware that many staff managers and employers discard résumés containing excellent material because they were poorly presented. Remember—your résumé, to do its job, must pass the "quick scan test."

To pass this test, your résumé must be visually inviting. Start by selecting a format. You will find some samples that have been successful beginning on page 78. Whether you choose one of these samples or create your own, be sure that the total effect is pleasing to the eye. Be equally sure that it is easy to read, and that the different sections are clearly separated from one another.

Separate thoughts into paragraphs with pleasing white space between them. There is nothing more difficult to scan than a long, solid block of text, with no breaks or indentations. Even better, itemize and highlight thoughts with dashes or asterisks. At the very least, separate each job by white space, providing different sections to the résumé.

Use good-quality paper and a clear, dark typewriter ribbon or cartridge. Make sure your typewriter's keys are clean, assuring you a clean, crisp copy. If you decide to use a paper color other than white, be sure it is a pastel that will contrast well with color of your type. (Beige paper with dark brown type is quite effective.) Avoid vibrant, bizarre, or otherwise loud, off-beat paper colors.

Use standard 8½ by 11-inch bond paper. It is a professional size, is easily handled, and is convenient to file. Avoid legal size paper, plastic sheet covers, or report folders—again, all too difficult to file. Keep away from unprofessional visual effects: photographs, illustrations, wild formats, or too many mixed-type styles.

Aim for one or two pages of typewritten material. Use only one side of the paper, and if the résumé is more than one page, staple the pages together, being sure that your name appears on each page.

Giving Your Résumé "Eye Appeal"

A professional layout should be subtle and unobtrusive, but at the same time it should direct the reader's eye to the most important information. You can accomplish this by using proper width margins, combining upper and lower case, underlining special items, as well as enclosing the entire résumé in a penned-in-border.

Use the ground—the white space on your paper—effectively. Use your margins imaginatively; use wide margins to lend importance to the information on the page and, at the same time, to provide a restful, easy-on-the-eye appearance. Create white space by double or triple spacing between blocks of information.

Be selective in your use of upper case; perhaps reserve it for job titles or names of employers. You might underline major accomplishments, but this, too, should be done sparingly. Avoid allowing your résumé to look too "busy," which is often what results when you use too many type faces and a plethora of underlines.

Reproduction

There was a time when employers expected every résumé to be individually typed. Fortunately, those days have passed. Although carbon or mimeograph copies are not acceptable (because of smudging and lack of clarity), any other duplicating process that turns out clear, sharp copies may be used.

Photocopying and offset printing give excellent results. Even Xerox copies are acceptable as long as they are sharp and clear. Offset printing should cost no more than a few dollars per one hundred copies, a relatively small price to pay for a crisp, professional-looking résumé.

Since the success of your job campaign very likely may hinge upon the appearance of your résumé, it is important that you have a superior product. Printing and copying services are listed in the telephone yellow pages under the heading "Offset Reproduction." Many of these services will also be able to retype your résumé and assist you with the layout and choice of available type faces.

Organizing Your Thoughts 4

Before you sit down to actually write your résumé, it is imperative that you organize all your information in terms of dates, education and courses, hardware and software, employers, job responsibilities, and all the other data that will be included. We've found that the most difficult part of writing a résumé is putting your thoughts and data into a meaningful form. To help you accomplish this, we have provided a series of workspaces: forms and worksheets that will force you to analyze your data and organize it to correspond with the standard résumé formats. Using these worksheets will force you to examine the natures of your previous jobs and your particular skills and strengths, and will pay off tremendously later on when you begin writing your résumé and when you have your job interviews. This chapter actually becomes a skeleton version of the first draft of your résumé.

Résumé Workspace

Use the space that follows to provide the information indicated.

Identifying Information
Complete the following information.

Name:_____
(If married woman, include married and maiden names.)

Address:_____
(Street and number, city, state, and zip code.)

Home Phone:_____
(Be sure to give area code.)

Business Phone:_____
(Be sure to give area code.)

Note: If your business phone is confidential, state that, for example:
        Business phone: (212) 555-1280 (confidential)

Résumé Capsule

The résumé capsule, as with the job objective, is an optional feature. However, one or the other must be used if you are trying to change careers. Use this space to write a résumé capsule, whether you decide to use it on your final résumé or not.

_____

_____

_____

_____

_____

_____

Educational History

List your education as you did your employment history, **in reverse chronological order**: your most advanced degree or your most recent education is first. Be sure to list all pertinent details—dates, degrees earned, educational institutions attended, and so on.

Advanced Degree
Dates:

From   To
(year)   (year)

_____
(Name of university)

_____   _____

_____
(Address of university)

Undergraduate Degree
Dates:

_____
(Degrees or credits earned)

From   To
(year)   (year)

_____
(Name of university)

_____   _____

_____
(Address of university)

_____
(Degree or credits earned)

_____   _____
(Major)   (Minor)

Computer-related courses:_____

_____

_____

_____

Job Objective

Remember, the job objective is **optional**. If used, keep it brief. The only time it **must** be used is if you are trying to change careers.

_____

_____

_____

_____

Hardware and software

Machines:_____

_____

Operating Systems:_____

_____

Languages:_____

_____

_____

TP Monitors or Access Methods:_____

_____

_____

Databases:_____

_____

_____

Other Utility Packages (Statistical, Libraries, Editors, etc.):__

_____

_____

_____

Clearance (if any):_____

_____

Employment History

Your employment history should be listed in **reverse chronological order.**

Name of Company:_____

Address of Company:_____

_____

_____

Job Title:_____

Dates: Description of Responsibilities:_____

From   To

(Month/Year)   (Month/Year)

_____   _____

_____

_____

_____

_____

_____

_____

_____

Name of Company:_____

Address of Company:_____

_____

_____

Job Title:_____

Dates: Description of Responsibilities:_____

From   To

(Month/Year)   (Month/Year)

_____   _____

_____

_____

_____

_____

_____

_____

_____

Name of Company:_____

Address of Company:_____

_____

_____

Job Title:_____

Dates: Description of Responsibilities:_____
From   To
(Month/Year) (Month/Year)

_____   _____   _____

_____

_____

_____

_____

_____

_____

Personal Information

Willing to Relocate:_____

Willing to Travel:_____

Hobbies or Interests:_____

_____

_____

_____

_____

Professional Memberships and Affiliations:_____

_____

_____

_____

_____

Publications and Major Achievements:_____

_____

_____

Foreign Languages or any other special skills:_____

_____

Military Service

From   To   Arm and Branch of Service:_____
(Month/Year) (Month/Year)

_____   _____   _____

_____

Highest Rank Achieved:_____

_____

Service Schools or Special Training:_____

_____

References

   Though the names of your references should **never** be included on your résumé, it is a good idea to assemble your data at the time you are preparing your résumé. Have a minimum of three people as references. It is advisable to include a statement that references will be furnished upon request.

Note: List the complete address—street and number, city, state, and zip code. Give area code with telephone number.

Name of Reference:_____

Position:_____

Company Affiliation:_____

Company Address:_____

_____

Business Phone and Extension:_____

Name of Reference:_____

Position:_____

Company Affiliation:_____

Company Address:_____

_____

Business Phone and Extension:_____

Name of Reference:_____

Position:_____

Company Affiliation:_____

Company Address:_____

_____

Business Phone and Extension:_____

Name of Reference:_____

Position:_____

Company Affiliation:_____

Company Address:_____

_____

Business Phone and Extension:_____

Sometimes it will be difficult to put into words the exact nature of your job. To help you do this, we have included some Employment History Worksheets, on pages 31-33.

Start with your current or most recent position and list every job you have held since you left school. (If your last year of school was three years ago or less, list all jobs you held during summers or during the school year that had anything to do with your intended career.) Account for all gaps in time between jobs. If you have held more than one position with the same company, use a separate page to detail each position.

Certain information on the worksheet will **not** appear on your résumé, such as salary information and reason for leaving. We suggest including them on the worksheet because questions about them may come up during the interviews, and you will be better prepared if you have thought about them in advance.

In completing these worksheets, consider each individual program or system or feature that you have worked with and exactly what your role was. It may help you to think about your typical day and what you do on an hour-by-hour basis. If you have any previous job descriptions or status reports, they might be helpful in refreshing your memory.

Employment History Worksheet

FIRM_____City_____State_____

Last Title_____From_____To_____*Last Salary_____

*Reason for leaving_____

Previous Title(s)_____From_____To_____*Salary_____

Program/System/Feature_____

_____

_____

Hardware/Software_____

_____

Your Role and Responsibilities_____

_____

_____

Most Important Achievement_____

_____

_____

Program/System/Feature_____

_____

_____

Hardware/Software_____

_____

Your Role and Responsibilities_____

_____

_____

Most Important Achievement_____

_____

_____

*These **do not** appear on your résumé

Employment History Worksheet

FIRM_____City_____State_____

Last Title_____From_____To_____*Last Salary_____

*Reason for leaving_____

Previous Title(s)_____From_____To_____*Salary_____

Program/System/Feature_____

_____

_____

Hardware/Software_____

_____

Your Role and Responsibilities_____

_____

_____

Most Important Achievement_____

_____

_____

Program/System/Feature_____

_____

_____

Hardware/Software_____

_____

Your Role and Responsibilities_____

_____

_____

Most Important Achievement_____

_____

_____

*These **do not** appear on your résumé

Employment History Worksheet

FIRM_____City_____State_____

Last Title_____From_____To_____*Last Salary_____

*Reason for leaving_____

Previous Title(s)_____From_____To_____*Salary_____

Program/System/Feature_____

_____

_____

Hardware/Software_____

_____

Your Role and Responsibilities_____

_____

_____

Most Important Achievement_____

_____

_____

Program/System/Feature_____

_____

_____

Hardware/Software_____

_____

Your Role and Responsibilities_____

_____

_____

Most Important Achievement_____

_____

_____

*These **do not** appear on your résumé

Linked up with identifying your responsibilities and portraying your previous jobs is the matter of using strong, descriptive words to describe those activities. Look over the list of words below to help you identify ones that reflect or describe your job responsibilities and/or accomplishments. Use these words as needed to complete the Employment History Worksheets.

A—accomplish, account, accumulate, acquire, activate, adhere, administer, advertise, advise, allocate, analyze, appraise, approve, arrange, assign, assist, assume, assure, audit, augment, authorize, automate

B—brought, budget, built

C—catalogue, change, code, collect, communicate, compare, compile, complete, compose, compute, conceive, concentrate, conduct, configure, consider, construct, consult, continue, contract, contribute, control, cooperate, coordinate, correct, correlate, create, credit

D—debug, decrease, define, delegate, delete, design, determine, develop, direct, disperse, display, distribute, document

E—edit, educate, emphasize, employ, engage, engineer, enhance, enlarge, ensure, establish, examine, execute, exercise, expand, expedite, extend, evaluate

F—fix, flowchart, forecast, functioned as, furnish

G—generate, grant, graph, guarantee

H—head, help, hire

I—implement, improve, include, inform, initialize, initiate, inspect, install, instruct, integrate, interface, interpret, interview, invent, investigate, involve, issue

J—join, justify

L—lease, lessen, load

M—maintain, manage, market, master, measure, meet, modify, monitor, motivate

N—negotiate, neutralize, normalize, notify

O—open, operate, orchestrate, organize, order

P—participate, perform, persuade, plan, post, prepare, present, process, procure, produce, program, project, promote, propose, protect, provide, publicize, purchase

Q—qualify, quantify

R—reclaim, recommend, reconstruct, recruit, release, report, represent, request, require, requisition, research, resequence, reshape, responsible for, retrain, retrieve, review, revise

S—schedule, screen, secure, select, sell, serve, set objectives, set up, solve, sort, specify, staff, standardize, stimulate, strengthen, structure, subcontract, submit, succeed, summarize, supervise, supply, support, synthesize, systematize

T—teach, test, trace, track, train, transfer, translate

U—update, upgrade, underscore, utilize

V—validate, verify, visualize

W—write

Developing a Successful Marketing Plan

5

You have followed the rules, and have a superior, hard-hitting résumé. Now, how are you to make the best possible use of it?

Moving Up

The most usual, and simplest, plan is to move up the ladder in a relatively straight line, assuming more and broader responsibilities as part of your job while staying in the same industry. Chances are you are looking for a position similar to the one now held by your boss.

The "how" to get the job you want is relatively straightforward. You must be in the right place at the right time. True, a certain amount of luck is involved, but most successful people make their own luck. It's more than luck when an individual sends a well-written résumé to an appropriate employer, obtains an interview, interviews successfully, and then is offered a job. That "lucky" person set the wheels in motion to get those positive results. In essence, that's the whole secret of job hunting: getting your résumé to the right place and then converting the interview into a job offer.

Though it is common knowledge that the computer industry is bursting with job opportunities, how do you find the one job that is perfect for you? Knowing what's out there obviously maximizes your chance of getting the job you want. To become more familiar with the opportunities that are open for you, consult the following sources:

- ☐ Employment agencies
- ☐ Newspaper ads
- ☐ "Networking"—among friends and colleagues
- ☐ Industry journals and newsletters
- ☐ Direct mail campaign or "cold calling"

Let's take them in turn.

Employment Agencies

An important source of job openings is the appropriate private employment agency. Since their only source of income is the fees paid by employers for successful job placements, it is in the agent's best interest to pursue this function in a diligent, aggressive manner. Private employment agencies recruit and screen applicants for many different companies and, therefore, are in a position to introduce you to a number of prospective employers.

Finding the appropriate agency is a very important consideration in the job hunt.

Read the classified section of your newspaper to find out if there are employment agencies in your area which either service or specialize in computer personnel. The best way of finding a really good agency is to call a few companies in which you would like to be employed and ask someone in the personnel department to recommend employment agencies used by that organization.

If you are at a high-management level, you may want to check out executive recruiters, who are likely to have positions available in your field and at your level. Write or call the American Management Association (135 W. 50th Street, New York, N.Y. 10020 (212) 586-8100) for a copy of their *Executive Employment Guide.* You can obtain a list of more than 125 nationwide executive recruiters (some with offices all over the world) including their addresses, phone numbers, fields covered, minimum salaries of positions handled, and an indication as to whether each accepts résumés or will be willing to set up an interview regarding opportunities in general; send $2 to the abovementioned A. M. A.

Once you have a list of the agencies you feel can be helpful to you, make an appointment, either by phone or with a letter, for a personal interview at the agency. It is more important to establish a rapport with a few agents than to make a career of interviewing with many agencies.

The interview with the counselor at the agency is almost as important as the job interview itself. This is the point at which you can be completely frank in describing exactly what your job requirements are in terms of salary, location, benefits, type of work, growth opportunities, and so on.

The agency will describe every opening they have currently listed which would be relevant to a person with your background, and leave you the choice of which ones you want to investigate further. Effectively, the agency does your legwork for you, and will keep you informed of new job openings as they arise. Most agencies expect and need résumés, and you should be prepared to give them several copies.

Almost every agency will, at a minimum, recopy your résumé onto their own letterhead. Many will make helpful suggestions about the content or style of your résumé, and frequently they will change the format to one which is standard for their agency. There are pluses and minuses when this happens. Since the agency uses its own paper and format, there will be nothing to distinguish your résumé from any other sent out by this agent. So forget about that special paper you may have picked out, or the particular type font you may have planned to use. In some cases, agents have actually hurt a candidate's chances by changes they made on the résumé. In one extreme case, the candidate's last name was omitted! In another case, the contents of the résumé were changed so radically that it no longer described the candidate. During the interview, one employer asked about something mentioned in the résumé and received the reply, "Oh, does it say I did *that*?"

On the other hand, a good agent can play a critical role in improving your résumé and getting that résumé in front of your prospective employer. The most important rule to follow when you work with an agent is to make sure that you see and approve the résumé that will actually be sent to the prospective employer.

Once the agent presents you with some leads for job openings, it's a good idea to be flexible in terms of which opportunities you are willing to investigate. For example, even though your background may be entirely research oriented and your intention is to continue in this direction, you may find an opportunity in the commercial world much more interesting than you imagined. In fact, frequently if the employer likes the applicant, the job might be redefined in terms of qualifications or salary. Of course, if you don't go on the interview that can never happen.

It is very important to check back with your counselor after every job interview. This will help the agent have more insight into your unique needs and requirements.

The agent can also play a large role in the salary negotiations once a job offer is to be made. It is always easier to have a third party represent you in negotiations for a higher salary or better conditions.

As mentioned earlier, the agency fees in the computer field are generally paid by the employer. However, don't hesitate to ask the agency interviewer to clarify any questions about your obligations. As with any other business arrangement, it is best to have a complete understanding of the terms at the very beginning of your relationship.

Newspaper Ads

Though it has been said that the odds of getting a job by responding to a newspaper ad are about equal to breaking the bank at Vegas, we disagree. We've known many people who get jobs—extremely good jobs—by this route. By all means, include responding to classified ads as part of your job campaign. You may be surprised to find that many of the ads which appear to be placed by employers actually come from employment agencies. You should respond to these just as you would to any other ad.

In general, most employment ads and services are listed in the classified sections of the Sunday local newspapers. However, it is important to study your daily newspapers to find their unique pattern for listing job opportunities. For instance, the *Wall Street Journal* features these ads every Tuesday, while the *New York Times* lists job opportunities in both their Sunday and Wednesday Business sections, as well as in the usual Classified columns. Because the *New York Times* Business section is circulated nationwide, while the Classified is distributed locally, the higher-level positions are more often placed in the Business section. Study both the Classified *and* Business sections of your newspapers.

As to which ads in particular to respond to, be sure to look under all the appropriate categories, and do it consistently. Some companies advertise by industry, others by function, still others by job title. A job opening for a Programmer might be found under the heading Computer Programmer, Data Processing, Application Programming, or simply Programmer. In some newspapers, there are no categories at all! For those instances, you must read through every ad on every page to find the openings which seem appropriate.

Start by responding to ads whose requirements are closest to your qualifications. Send an individually typed cover letter and a copy of your résumé. We suggest you answer every ad that you feel you are capable of handling, regardless of whether you have all the stated requirements, since employers are usually more flexible than their advertisements would imply. For example, assume an ad specifies that a candidate must have a minimum of one year of Cobol programming experience on payroll systems. We have seen cases where such jobs have been filled by people with experience in payroll systems without any actual programming experience. Likewise, we have seen such jobs filled by programmers who do not have payroll system experience. Ads usually describe the ideal candidate, just as applicants look for the ideal job. But in reality, both will compromise.

Keep a record of the date you answered each ad and continue on your job search (see page 43). You should call the personnel department about a week after you respond to the ad, and try to arrange an interview. Naturally, if you are responding to an ad which gave only a box number this will not be possible.

Networking

Networking is a new word for a process that job seekers have used since we evolved from feudal times and individuals sought employment. It's simply letting people know you're looking for a job and asking them for any leads they might know about. Of all the various job sources, the most convenient—and at times, the best—are your friends, relatives, and colleagues. If you are still employed, naturally you should be discrete with your current employer and immediate colleagues. However, an integral part of your campaign is to let as many people as possible know that you are job hunting.

Don't be embarrassed by asking for suggestions. Everyone you know has been in your position and knows that any help is appreciated. Were the positions reversed and a friend asked for help, wouldn't you be willing to assist in any way you could?

In addition to friends and colleagues, put yourself in situations in which you are apt to meet people who could help you. Likely places to meet such people are at computer classes, user group meetings, and conferences. Organizations such as the ACM, IEEE, SHARE, and the NCC are all fertile territory for making contacts. University alumni groups, fraternity brothers, and professional organizations have always provided men with an ideal nucleus for the "old buddy" system—a close group guaranteed to provide mutual support. Raised to its highest, most organized form, this systematic contacting is now called "networking" and is no longer limited to men.

Most female executives and professionals are great "networkers." Because of previous and on-going sexual discrimination, women have learned to cope and scramble in an alien world, a bit like a new immigrant trying to assimilate into a new culture. As a result, they are not reluctant to ask the right questions of anyone who might help them break down barriers.

Often people working in a particular company hear of job openings before the jobs are advertised or listed with employment agencies and recruiters, and are actually given a bonus if a candidate they recommend is hired. The typical employer feels more secure about an applicant referred by someone he or she knows than an individual recruited from a newspaper ad or from commercial recruiters.

If you hear about a job opening in a particular company or believe one is about to occur, use your contacts to find out who knows somebody in power. Don't hesitate to ask a friend to introduce you to the proper person.

Though job hunters have always elicited the help of friends, the technique of networking is only now beginning to spread. A noted former radical, excoriated in the sixties by a large segment of society for his anti-establishment behavior, helped broaden the networking concept in the early eighties by taking over a large New York discotheque in offnights. By promising both professional and social introductions to the attending men and women, he generated the exchange of thousands of business cards, leading to proposals of various kinds—many of them jobs.

Business and Trade Publications

Allocate several hours a week for time at your public library to read trade journals and business magazines. You'll want to assemble a system effective enough for you to anticipate trends which are likely to trigger job openings. Read magazines and newspapers such as *Computerworld, Information News, Datamation, Electronic News,* and *Byte* on a regular basis to make yourself an expert on current business information. Check the back-of-the-magazine classified ads for openings you might want to follow up.

In all probability you've read ads of the many career service organizations offering you access to the hundreds of job opportunities that are never advertised. These services offer, for a fee of several thousand dollars, to give you a method of contacting this vast market. Their ads are convincing. But is it worth the money?

There are, in fact, a tremendous number of opportunities in the hidden job market. It has been estimated that 90 percent of the job openings filled each year have never been advertised nor have they been listed with either an employment agency or an executive recruiter. They were filled by individuals who either tapped into the network or made contact with the particular employer by sending an unsolicited résumé.

The major contribution of these high-priced career services is the assistance they offer in conducting a direct mail campaign. By initiating your own campaign you can get the same results and save yourself a bundle of money.

Because the computer industry is enjoying such rapid expansion, this is the ideal time to get positive results from a properly executed direct mail campaign. If an individual with computer experience sends a résumé to twenty-five companies it is probable that twenty of them will have a job opening at the present time.

Using this method of job hunting has another advantage. You take the active role. You choose the companies that interest you rather than passively answering ads as they appear.

Obviously, your résumé will be an integral part of this campaign. Since you have already prepared the best possible résumé, you are ready to start. Your next step is to compile a list of potential employers. Possible sources for your list of companies could be the Yellow Pages of the telephone book, newspaper ads (even though they may not be advertising jobs for which you qualify), organizational membership lists, business directories, financial directories, trade journals, and magazines.

Learn as much as possible about the companies you have chosen. Research them thoroughly. Find out the names and titles of their officers, the number and location of branch offices, the nature of their products or service, and any information regarding acquisitions, mergers, or expansions. Such information is readily available in a variety of business directories which can be found in your local library. Directories exist for every field.

Read current and back issues of such trade journals as *Computerworld, Datamation Electronic News,* and gather more information on exciting companies. This research will help you decide which companies interest you enough to be on your list.

The list of prospective companies should not be too long. Though you're looking for a minimum of facts, you don't want to feel that you have involved yourself in an interminable project. Bear in mind that every company on your list must receive your résumé accompanied by an individually typed cover letter addressed to the appropriate person. You should, if at all possible, determine the name and title of the person you plan to be your addressee. Reference books such as *Standard & Poors* can give you this information.

The remainder of your direct mail campaign involves the actual mailing of the résumés and cover letters and the follow up with phone calls. We've already spoken about the follow-up phone call; don't neglect it, because it may be the thing that will prod the employer to set up an interview with you. You initiate the action. **Don't wait for them to call.** Your making the call prevents your letter from remaining unanswered and at the same time gives a more **professional, aggressive impression.**

Keep a record of each résumé sent and note the dates of your calls and interviews. Also indicate the results of each call and interview, and remember your follow-up letters. Don't leave anything to your memory; maintain a written record.

The simplest way of maintaining a record of your direct mail campaign, answers to classified ads, or résumés mailed through personal contacts is to make a carbon copy of each covering letter as you type it. On the bottom of the carbon, you can note date and result of your follow-up phone call, date of interview, result of interview, and follow-up note. These can be kept in a file folder with a separate sheet—or calendar page— with dates and times of interviews noted. It would be disastrous to set up two interviews for the same time.

A second system is to set up a large sheet of paper with column headings across the top of the sheet. The information, of course, would be the same as that maintained by using carbon copies. Below is the suggested heading for each column. The headings would be separated by lines drawn vertically down the full length of the sheet, and horizontal lines would be drawn, each about two inches below the other, to separate the entries for each company written. I suggest the following headings:

Résumé Mailing	Follow-Up Phone Call	Interview	Thank-You Letter	Job Offer	Confirmation or "No Thank You, But" Letter
Name	Date	Date	Date	Yes	Date
Title	Results	Time		No	Letter Type
Company		Interviewer			
Address		Results			
Date Sent					

Résumé Mailing

Name _____

Title _____

Company _____

Address _____

Date Sent _____

Follow-Up Phone Call

Date _____

Results _____

_____

_____

Interview

Date _____

Time _____

Interviewer _____

Results _____

Thank-You Letter

Date _____

Job Offer

Yes _____

No _____

Confirmation or "No Thank You, But" Letter

Date _____

Letter Type _____

Résumé Mailing

Name _____

Title _____

Company _____

Address _____

Date Sent _____

Follow-Up Phone Call

Date _____

Results _____

_____

_____

Interview

Date _____

Time _____

Interviewer _____

Results _____

Thank-You Letter

Date _____

Job Offer

Yes _____

No _____

Confirmation or "No Thank You, But" Letter

Date _____

Letter Type _____

Résumé Mailing

Name _____

Title _____

Company _____

Address _____

Date Sent _____

Follow-Up Phone Call

Date _____

Results _____

_____

_____

Interview

Date _____

Time _____

Interviewer _____

Results _____

Thank-You Letter

Date _____

Job Offer

Yes _____

No _____

Confirmation or "No Thank You, But" Letter

Date _____

Letter Type _____

Résumé Mailing

Name _____

Title _____

Company _____

Address _____

Date Sent _____

Follow-Up Phone Call

Date _____

Results _____

_____

_____

Interview

Date _____

Time _____

Interviewer _____

Results _____

Thank-You Letter

Date _____

Job Offer

Yes _____

No _____

Confirmation or "No Thank You, But" Letter

Date _____

Letter Type _____

Résumé Mailing

Name _____

Title _____

Company _____

Address _____
_____

Date Sent _____

Follow-Up Phone Call

Date _____

Results _____
_____
_____

Interview

Date _____

Time _____

Interviewer _____

Results _____

Thank-You Letter

Date _____
_____

Job Offer

Yes _____

No _____

Confirmation or "No Thank You, But" Letter

Date _____

Letter Type _____

Résumé Mailing

Name _____

Title _____

Company _____

Address _____
_____

Date Sent _____

Follow-Up Phone Call

Date _____

Results _____
_____
_____

Interview

Date _____

Time _____

Interviewer _____

Results _____

Thank-You Letter

Date _____
_____

Job Offer

Yes _____

No _____

Confirmation or "No Thank You, But" Letter

Date _____

Letter Type _____

KEEPING RECORDS

Résumé Mailing

Name _____
Title _____
Company _____
Address _____
_____
Date Sent _____

Follow-Up Phone Call

Date _____
Results _____
_____
_____

Interview

Date _____
Time _____
Interviewer _____
_____
Results _____

Thank-You Letter

Date _____
_____

Job Offer

Yes _____
No _____

Confirmation or "No Thank You, But" Letter

Date _____
Letter Type _____
_____

Résumé Mailing

Name _____
Title _____
Company _____
Address _____
_____
Date Sent _____

Follow-Up Phone Call

Date _____
Results _____
_____
_____

Interview

Date _____
Time _____
Interviewer _____
_____
Results _____

Thank-You Letter

Date _____
_____

Job Offer

Yes _____
No _____

Confirmation or "No Thank You, But" Letter

Date _____
Letter Type _____
_____

The third system involves the use of 4 × 6-inch index cards. Again, the information would be the same as the other systems. Below is a sample layout for the card:

Mr. Richard Rowe   Mailed 3/22/84
Chief Draftsman
Systems, Inc.
424 Park Place
Buford, Pa. 21370

Phone Call: _____
                              (indicate date)

(Note results) _____

Interview: _____
                         (indicate date, time, and interviewer)

(Note results) _____

Thank-You Letter _____
                              (indicate date)

Job Offer _____

Confirmation *or* "No Thank You, But" Letter _____
                                                      (indicate date and letter type)

This system is best for a very large mailing. We suggest that you have the index cards printed up cheaply rather than trying to type them yourself.

Keeping a record of your job campaign is worth the effort it takes. Especially when you are involved with a large mailing, it is the only way of insuring that you will be able to keep track of which companies you have contacted and what the results were. Aside from eliminating the chances of sending a résumé to the same company twice, or of making two interview appointments for the same time, it provides a useful means of reviewing the progress of your job campaign at any give time.

The Cover Letter

6

A covering letter should be enclosed every time you send out your résumé. Its enclosure is not only an act of courtesy but a means of adding a personal touch. It gives each individual you approach an indication of your personal attention to his or her situation—which would not be the case if the résumé arrived unaccompanied. The covering letter also neutralizes the tone of the impersonal, reproduced résumé.

This is your chance to let your individual style, personality, and unique strengths stand out from the crowd. Don't be afraid to "sell" yourself here by describing some unique incident or experience. If you wish to do something flamboyant, the cover letter, rather than the résumé, is the place to do it.

Our corporate experts tell us they are much more likely to read a résumé accompanied by a covering letter than one received without a letter. The letter removes the look of a mass mailing.

It doesn't matter whether you are sending your résumé in answer to an ad, to an employment agency, or as part of your personal mailing campaign. The cover letter will always follow the same, simple rules. It should be brief—limited to one page and no more than four paragraphs. Needless to say, it should be neatly typed, and conform to the standards of business correspondence.

Whenever possible, address the letter to a particular individual in the company, preferably by name and title. If it is impossible to ascertain the name, address the letter to "Personnel Director" or, by title, to the head of the department in which you are hoping to work. In answering an ad, however, address your letter as the ad indicates. If there is no more than a box number, simply address it to that box number.

The first paragraph of your letter is the most important, since it may determine whether or not the reader continues to read. Just as in a newspaper article, the first sentence or "lead" should be original and informative, and it should set the tone for the rest of the letter. It should tell why you are writing to that particular person or company. If it is in answer to an ad, say so, and give the name and date of the publication where the ad appeared. If the letter is part of your direct mail campaign, explain in two or three lines either why you would like to work for that particular company or why you feel their hiring you would be in their company's best interest. A frequent mistake in cover letters is to describe why the job is in the candidate's best interest, rather than to stress what the candidate can do for the employer. For example, to say "I believe your firm can offer me the dynamic challenges and responsibilities I seek" does not convince a recruiter of what you have to offer that company.

If a friend who is an employee has suggested you make contact with this particular company, you should give the name, title or job category, and the department where the friend is employed.

Some typical opening lines are:

> "Dorothy Johnson, a programmer in the systems programming department, suggested that I write to you."

> "I am replying to your ad which appeared in the New York *Times* on Sunday, May 12th."

> "Your recent acquisition of C & M Computers Company led me to believe you might be interested in my nine years experience as a systems analyst."

The following one or two paragraphs should point out the salient features of your résumé which could be of interest to your correspondent. These paragraphs are the very guts of your covering letter. In a sentence or two, tell why you would be an asset to the company receiving your letter. Succinctly lay out your credentials, and refer to your accomplishments, skills, or areas of expertise. In certain circumstances, you might elaborate on one or two entries on your résumé.

Use the cover letter to describe special projects in which you played a key role, or the features of a program you worked on which were unusual. Another frequent use of the cover letter is to summarize your achievements in a somewhat more readable form than the optional Summary portion of the résumé.

Because different aspects of your résumé are highlighted in each cover letter, the same résumé can be used to pursue different job opportunities. The covering letter, stressing your most appropriate skills and talents, can be geared uniquely to each particular company that will be the recipient of your résumé.

The last paragraph should be the closing, indicating your hope that you have created interest in yourself, your wish to thank the reader for his or her consideration, and your suggestion that you will call shortly to arrange an interview. Unless you are replying to a box number ad, always state that you will initiate the action to obtain an interview.

Taking the initiative is important. Saying you will call to set up a date for the interview increases your chances of getting it. Essential as it is for employers to recruit the best people, the press of day-to-day responsibilities often pushes this need down the list of professional priorities. Because enough candidates will call to set up interviews, it is very likely the job will be filled before the employer can take the necessary action to set up a series of appointments.

Types of Cover Letters

There are several situations which require you to mail your résumé and cover letter. These are:

☐ A response to an ad.

☐ An unsolicited inquiry to a targeted employer as part of your direct mail campaign.

☐ A letter to a friend or colleague who might offer assistance in a job search.

☐ A letter to an employment agency.

Response to an Ad

Read the ads carefully, marking or clipping those of interest to you. Examine the requirements thoroughly. As we mentioned before, employers advertise for the "ideal" candidate and, more often than not, actually hire an individual not possessing every qualification listed in the original ad. For that reason, it is a good idea to reply not only to those ads which fit you perfectly, but also to those for which you meet just some of the requirements.

Now re-read each ad you intend to answer. Study each separately. Assume that the requirements are rank ordered, and deal with each as sequenced in the ad. List on a piece of scratch paper every qualification, skill, strength, or accomplishment you possess relevant to the particular advertisement. If you don't have all the requirements, make a note of any experience in either your education or work history that demonstrates other capabilities which would make you an asset to that particular company. Write and re-write this information until you have eliminated all excess words. Communicate your strengths clearly and succintly. Work on your letter until each idea flows effortlessly to the next. Let's look at a typical ad and consider how to respond to it.

COMPUTER OPERATOR

Will maintain and operate hardware used in advanced computer research. This individual will identify problems and interact with programmers. The position involves loading of jobs and monitoring the progress of the system. Requires 1-2 years' related experience, including familiarity with DEC and/or IBM. A graduate of a computer technical school is desirable.

Join an exciting high-tech environment with excellent benefits and growth potential. Send résumé and salary history to John Reed, Personnel Representative, RCA Corporation of America, Department 462153, 320 E. 20 Street, New York, N.Y. 10028.

An Equal Opportunity Employer

RCA Corporation
of
America

An appropriate reply can be found on page 57. Address your letter to the company and person listed in the ad, or simply to the Personnel Director if no individual's name is listed.

It's a good idea to research each company whose ad you intend to answer, and then include in your letter any new information you have become aware of: an expansion, recent or imminent merger, acquisition, or new product developments or services. Mention how you would be able to help the organization implement or maximize its current goals. (Obviously, if the ad only lists a box number, this will not be possible.)

Don't be discouraged if you don't get an immediate response. We've found it is not unusual for a recruiter to hold résumés for more than six weeks before setting up interviews.

An effective method of making certain your résumé will be noticed is to write your cover letter in the form of a mailgram. This guarantees a certain exclusivity, especially when answering an ad which is likely to attract a plethora of résumés. This is one situation where you must not be shy. Don't be afraid to take the initiative; telephone the personnel director or even the staff manager, if you know his or her name, to arrange a time for a personal interview.

Direct Mail Letter

A successful technique in a job campaign is to select a number of employers of your choice and simply send each a copy of your résumé with an individually written cover letter. As we mentioned earlier, compile a list of prospective employers using professional journals, business directories, and other references. Learn as much as possible about the companies you have chosen. In particular, you want to find out what type of hardware, software, and application systems the company uses, to see if there is a match with your background. This may not be easily determined from library research, but a few well-placed phone calls can frequently give you the answers you need.

These days it is safe to assume that almost any company will have some kind of computer facility, or at least a few personal computers. Most large companies will have a data processing (DP) department and/or management information systems (MIS) department, and a computer operations group. A bold but effective strategy is to call the company switchboard and ask for the Director of Computer Operations. He or she will certainly be in a position to know what hardware and software the company is using. Politely state your name and reason for calling, and simply ask what computer systems the company uses. You may be surprised to get a wealth of information, which will be invaluable to you in formulating your letter of inquiry. Or you may find out that the company uses a kind of hardware or software which is completely foreign to you. In that case, you may want to target your campaign to another company. If you strike out with the Director of Operations, try the Manager of Information Processing, Data Processing or Information Center. By finding out this valuable information before mailing a barrage of letters, you can save yourself a great deal of trouble.

Don't let this research overwhelm you; you're looking for a minimum of facts. If you are planning to send out fifty or more letters, research the ten or twelve companies in which you have the most interest. For the remaining organizations, it is enough to simply address the letter to the appropriate person and then mention the company name once or twice in the body of your letter. In essence, you are trying to make the letter appear as personal as possible, bearing in mind that most people don't read *form* letters.

In each letter point out the particular strengths and accomplishments that would be of interest to the reader and indicate where they are described in your résumé. The tone of the letter should generate interest in you. Refer to a particular qualification that will demonstrate why it would be particularly advantageous to the potential employer to add you to its staff. Always discuss how you can be of value to them rather than how they can help you. Close by a courteous thank-you, and state that you will call in a few days to set up an appointment.

Letter to a Colleague or Friend

Colleagues, friends, or relatives can often be an excellent source of leads. For that reason, you should give them a copy of your résumé. When sending your résumé, include a short informal note instead of a businesslike covering letter. The note should simply say that you're in the process of seeking employment or attempting to change jobs and would appreciate any suggestions he or she can offer. You might mention how you feel about relocation, and if your job search is confidential, make sure you mention that. Don't discuss your salary requirements, but you might ask if it would be useful to send additional résumés.

Letters to Employment Agencies

Start by calling each target employment agency and executive search firm in your area, and talking with—or get the name of—the highest ranking individual. In some cases, you might set up a meeting; in other instances, you'll get "permission" to send your résumé. For the out-of-town agencies or to those whose names are unavailable, simply address your covering letter to the president.

The purpose of your letter is to set up a conversation with the appropriate recruiter in each agency—best done in person; second best by phone. Request your résumé be kept on file so that you can be notified of any suitable job openings. Though we recommend that you discuss your feelings concerning relocation, the covering letter is not the place to mention salary requirements. You should keep your cover letter brief, but at the same time make reference to certain of your strengths.

Since executive recruiters re-write résumés, (not always to the candidate's advantage), **you must ask them to show you your "re-written" résumé before it is sent to a potential employer.** We cannot emphasize this too strongly!

The last paragraph, similar to the other types of cover letters, should include an indication that you will phone in a week or so to set up either a phone or a personal interview.

19 Windfield Drive
Cleveland, Ohio 44110
October 3, 1984

Miss Lee Harris
Personnel Representative
Esso Oil, Inc.
Cambridge, MA 02142

Dear Miss Harris:

I enclose my résumé in response to your advertisement in the Sunday, Oct. 2 Cleveland Plain Dealer. I am interested in the position of Senior Technical Writer.

I believe I have the ability to produce clear, effective prose on a deadline. Last fall I began writing for Biochemists in a field completely new to me. In less than one year, I researched and wrote a 225-page history of Glycoproteins, a technical manual on the isolation and characteristics of Glycoproteins used by the Clinical Chemists at Cleveland General Hospital. In addition I decoded and rewrote many papers on topics ranging from Protein Chemistry and Cancer to the Biochemistry of Embryogenesis. These projects are hard evidence of my strong writing skills and ability to grasp and clearly explain technically complex subjects.

I enter the electronics field with more knowledge than I entered medicine, as I studied computer science and related subjects in college. Making technical subjects understandable and interesting for the most inexperienced person is my goal: technical material need not be as hard to digest as cold oatmeal, but should slip down like Mom's chicken soup.

I will call in 2 weeks to answer any questions you might have and to set up an appointment at your convenience. Thank you for your consideration.

Sincerely,

Bette Smith

Bette Smith

Enclosure

Anne Newman
405 West End Ave.
N.Y., N.Y. 10023
March 6, 1984

M104 Globe Office
Boston Globe
Boston, Ma. 02107

Ladies/Gentlemen:

In the interest of investigating employment opportunities with your
organization, I have enclosed a copy of my résumé for your review.
It will furnish you with specific information relative to my professional background, experiences, and capabilities.

I am seeking a position as a D.P. Manager where a diverse and hands-
on training background would assist your company in achieving its
goals. As my resume indicates, I have had an extensive background
in Computer Operations and have gained thorough experience with
supervision and training of personnel.

I am now interested in leaving my present position and applying these
background skills and business abilities in a challenging, professional
environment.

Realizing, however, that this summary statement cannot adequately
communicate my experiences in-depth, I would appreciate having the
opportunity to discuss with you in person how my qualifications would
benefit your firm. I look forward to talking with you.

Sincerely,

Anne Newman

Anne Newman

Résumé Enclosed

Charles Sherman
16 Pine St.
Philadelphia, Pa 01623
(215) 621-9684
November 5, 1984

Mr. John Reed
Personnel Representative
RCA Corporation of America
Department 462153
320 E. 20 Street
N.Y., N.Y. 10028

Dear Mr. Reed:

Please find the enclosed résumé in response to your advertisement for
a computer operator, which appeared in the New York Times, Sunday,
November 4, 1984.

Please note that I am a recent CDP Graduate and have received hands-on
training with IBM Hardware, specifically the 4331 DOS/VSE. While I am
trained as a Computer Programmer, and am indeed pursuing my career in
this direction, Computer Operations is a side benefit of my training,
and I do in fact have over one year's experience, hands-on, in this Hardware environment.

My portfolio contains various samples of Applications and IMS program
development utilizing POWER, JCL, and the various support utilities of
the 370 Operating System. I would be able to present this portfolio
for your inspection at the time of an interview, and would look forward
to the opportunity to do so.

I believe I can bring to your corporation the benefits of maturity,
stability, and the ability to contribute through growth in a long-term
commitment.

I am currently doing Consulting and Software Design work on a contract
basis in the White Plains, New York area, and have had to increase my
skills to include familiarity with the Digital VAX/VMS & RSX-11 impli-
mentations being used extensively in this area. As this work necessitates
frequent visits to the New York area, I would be able to meet with you at
any time to discuss this matter further.

I look forward to hearing from you as I am genuinely interested in this
position.

Very truly yours,

Charles Sherman

Charles Sherman

Enclosure

10 Slate St. #216
Lawrence, N.Y. 11557
February 8, 1985

Paul Barron
Apple Computers, Inc.
15 Harris St.
Silver Springs, Md. 20550

Dear Mr. Barron:

I read about Apple, Inc., in your recent advertisement in the
Washington Post. I am interested in a technical consultant
position with your marketing department. I believe my teaching
and software development experience is suitable for Apple Computers, Inc.

As my enclosed résumé indicates, I graduated from Yale University
with a degree in computer science, and am currently employed as a
software engineer. In this capacity I have developed a management information system and implemented phases of a high-level
graphics language compiler. In addition to my technical background, I have taught computer science concepts to both engineers
and college students. During the past six months I developed a
curriculum and taught an in-house graphics language seminar.
Furthermore, I just completed my fourth year of teaching an introductory programming course at Yale University.

I see a good fit between my qualifications and the needs of your
company. I would appreciate the opportunity to discuss with you
how I could contribute to Apple Computers, Inc., and will call
within the next two weeks to set up an appointment.

Sincerely,

James Brightwell

James Brightwell

Encl.

78 Winchester Street
Cleveland, Ohio 44112

March 12, 1984

Dear Paul,

I ran into Roger Whitcomb at SHARE last month. He told me about
some of the work you've been doing at Varian and suggested that
I get in touch with you. Tricia will be finishing her intern-
ship in June and we have decided to look for jobs in the San
Francisco Bay area.

Since we last saw you, I've been promoted to Lead Programmer/
Analyst at Calico Systems, working on the General Ledger and
Accounts Receivable Systems. I've also been working at home on
my PC and have become a pretty fair "C" programmer. So, I'm
open to positions in either the micro or the mainframe arenas.

I'd really appreciate any suggestions you might have that could
be helpful in finding a job. If there are any agencies you feel
are particularly good, let me know about them also.

I've enclosed three copies of my résumé. Feel free to circulate
them as you see fit.

Tricia and I will be coming out on a job-hunting expedition next
month. I'm looking forward to seeing you.

Sincerely,

Larry

56 Mountain View Rd.
Skokie, Ill.   60076

November 8, 1984

Mr. Richard Carter
C. & S. Electronics, Inc.
Chicago, Ill.   60071

Dear Mr. Carter,

Bill Casey, an employee of the C. & S. Electronics and a long-time friend, recently informed me of an opening for a technical writer at your company. I would like to apply for that position, and I have enclosed a copy of my résumé for your consideration.

At the present time I am a Social Worker working at the Gateway Foundation counseling mentally handicapped adults. However, I wish to make a career change to a field where my intellectual talents can be challenged and broadened in new areas. Technical writing, with its challenge in concise expression and its relation to teaching through technical documents, is the field which appeals to me.

As for my background for this position, I have a great deal of experience in writing. I have edited and written a newsletter for Midwestern Clinical Social Workers for two years. During my academic career in liberal arts, I wrote two theses and innumerable papers. I have also published two papers on Clinical Social Work, and I was recently contracted to write an article for a magazine for college students. As a Social Worker and Counselor I have learned to communicate to diverse audiences. As a result, I am familiar not only with the proper technical facets of writing but also with the techniques of expressing ideas to a variety of people.

Although I do not have formal training in electrical engineering or computer programming, I have a strong interest in those fields. I have completed the six-month course at the Chicago Institute for Computer Programming, with very high grades. Finally, I am a quick learner, and I am willing to add to my knowledge of computers to aid my skills in technical writing. Therefore, I hope you will consider me for a position with C. & S. Electronics, Inc. as a technical writer. I will call next week to set up an interview at your convenience.

Sincerely,

Donald McBride
Donald McBride

encl.

76 Arlington Road
Fort Worth, TX 76105
June 23, 1984

Ms. Roberta D'Angelo
Career Placements, Inc.
753 Seventh Avenue
Burlington, MA 01803

Dear Ms. D'Angelo:

Thank you for taking the time to discuss opportunities available to me through Career Placement. As I mentioned in our conversation, I feel my strengths are in the areas of software tools and kernel operating systems. A copy of my résumé is enclosed detailing this experience.

I have most recently been working on a project involving a UNIX based filing system on a 68000 based processor. I was responsible for the test support tools and database verifier.

I am particularly interested in a start-up venture offering an equity position. I am open to relocation anywhere in the New England area.

I look forward to an interview where I can review my background and possible opportunities with you in person.

Sincerely,

Julie Shriber

Julie Shriber

35 Main Street
Newark, N.J. 07841

May 10, 1984

Ms. Dorothy Eaton
Davis Research Systems
Personnel Department
19 Center Street
New York, N.Y. 10016

Dear Ms. Eaton:

John Davis, of your Washington, D.C. office, suggested that
I send my résumé to you. As you may be aware, John and I
worked together when he was employed by Wang, Inc.

One item not specifically mentioned in the résumé, and which
may be of interest, is the fact that I have designed and
written three user functions for Wang's version of System
1022. All functions were written as standard callable modules
with the actual function simply obtaining the arguments, and
creating the environment in which to call the desired module.
When control is received back, the function re-establishes the
System 1022 environment and returns the results to the user.
This approach allows the module which does the actual work to
be used by both System 1022 and other languages.

I look forward to meeting you in the near future and will call
you early next week.

Yours truly,

Diane Wilson

Diane Wilson

Enclosure

81 Hobart St.
San Francisco, CA 94110
(415) 872-6140
Nov. 15, 1983

Mr. Kenneth Rivers
Personnel Department
Alpha Computers, Inc.
910 N. Lemon Ave.
Orlando, FL 32800

Dear Mr. Rivers:

In January 1984, I will receive my Bachelor of Arts degree in Computer
Science from UCLA. I am interested in obtaining a programming position
in a software development firm beginning in February.

Friends have told me about Alpha International and, after investigation,
I have discovered that Alpha is exactly the type of company I would like
to work for. A friend gave me the name of Ms. Dorothy Harris with whom
I spoke yesterday. She suggested that I forward my résumé to you and
said that in the meantime she would discuss setting up an interview in
the near future.

I have worked for the UCLA Office of University Information Systems for
three years, part time during school and full time through the summers
and other vacations. My most recent work has been in COBOL, although I
have programmed in ADABAS NATURAL and done some maintenance to Assembler
programs.

I know that Alpha does much of its development in Assembler. This
furthers my interest in the company, as Assembler is one of my strongest
languages and I enjoy programming in it. I am now taking my third Assembler course at UCLA, in which I will write an operating system for the
IBM 3081.

I look forward to speaking with you and will call next week.

Sincerely,

Hilda Majors

Hilda Majors

Enclosure

26 James Street
Chicago, Illinois 60602
April 6, 1984

Mr. John Anderson
Personnel Director
Digital Corporation
Detroit, Michigan 51073

Dear Mr. Anderson:

I am a graduate student in Computer Science at Yale University, and I will be awarded an M.S. degree in June 1984. I am currently looking for a position related to Database/Graphics Package Design in the research and development department of a major company.

Before coming to Yale, I designed, supervised, and completed a CAD system. The function covers vector, character and curve generation, windowing, shading, and transformations.

At Yale, my research work involves Compilation of Relational Queries into Network DML. To enhance my background, I have taken some courses in Computer Graphics and Data Base, and I have experience in and understanding of the design of Database. With this strong background, I certainly believe that I am competent to meet challenging tasks and can make a good contribution to your company.

Enclosed please find my résumé, which indicates in some detail my training and experience. I sincerely hope that my qualifications are of interest to you and that an interview might be arranged at your convenience.

Thank you for your consideration and I am looking forward to hearing from you soon.

Sincerely yours,

Martha Levine

Martha Levine

Encl.

410 Hunter Avenue
Grand Rapids, MI   48505

September 14, 1983

Ms. Emily Turner
Apple Computers, Inc.
50 Broad St.
Dallas, Texas 75214

Dear Ms. Turner:

If you are looking for a computer programmer who sets unusually high
standards for herself, then I believe you will be interested in the
enclosed résumé.

By far the greatest satisfaction in my computer programming assignments to date has come from coaxing superior performance from the
hardware and software assigned to me. I have learned that some
remarkable and highly rewarding results are produced when an energetic drive to find better methods in data processing is coupled with
due concern for costs and the needs of the people who work with me.

I like what I hear about your company. If you think, as I do, that
I can make a great contribution to your computer programming division,
I hope you won't mind a call next week to set a time to see you.

                                        Very truly yours,

                                        Anne Olson

                                        Anne Olson

Enclosure

Robert McLean
110 Devoe Ave.
Yonkers, N.Y. 10071
October 31, 1984

Mr. Robert Ludlow
System Services Corporation
510 Fifth Avenue
N.Y.C., N.Y. 10036

Dear Mr. Ludlow:

I believe that I am well qualified for the position of a
Database Designer in distributed DBMS, CAD/CAM DBMS, or
database support for large applications systems.

I have in-depth knowledge of database management technology
which includes the general DBMS, database organizations,
semantic data mondels, and distributed database systems; I
have good working experience in data definition language,
data manipulation language, and schema design; I have been
involved in the applications of the following popular commercial DBMS Systems: IMS, System 2000, and INGRES; what's more,
I have had over ten years of intensive experience in computer
applications in both business and engineering environments;
finally, I want to devote myself to the field of database
design.

I strongly believe that I can contribute a great deal to the
Database design project. I therefore enclose a copy of my
résumé, which further details the background I have in database design. It would be my pleasure to hear from you regarding this unique employment opportunity at System Services
Corporation.

Sincerely,

Robert McLean

Robert McLean

Encl.

Carl Fergerson
16 South Street
Darien, Connecticut 06490
February 8, 1984

Ms. Patricia Schwartz
Taft Computer Company
1800 Broad Street
Philadelphia, Pennsylvania 20171

Dear Patricia:

Thank you for taking the time to chat with me today. I have enclosed
my résumé, so that it may be circulated to the appropriate department
heads, when you contact them.

As we discussed today, I am interested in working for Taft in the
Philadelphia area and in dealing with customers. An experienced software
specialist, I have proposed, planned, designed, managed, developed, and
delivered major software systems to users. Project management of a multi-
person effort has been the primary responsibility of my latest job. In
addition to having management and technical skills, I enjoy people, giving
presentations, and consulting. Taft appears to offer opportunities in
marketing, customer support, and development that would use my computing
expertise, along with my verbal abilities.

Having recently delivered a significant software application, I would
like to begin a new challenge as soon as possible. I am also interested
in exploring positions in the research area, if you think there is a match.

I am looking forward to hearing from you soon, and establishing the next
step in our discussion. I will call next week to set up our next meeting.

Talking with you was a pleasure and has given me a very positive impression
of Taft as a company.

Yours truly,

Carl Fergerson

Carl Fergerson

encl.

79 Coastal Highway
Miami Beach, Florida 33110
September 7, 1984

Mr. Marc Thomas
Leisure Realty Corporation
Miami, Florida 33133

Dear Mr. Thomas,

I just wanted to write to tell you how pleased I was to meet with
you last Wednesday.

I was particularly impressed by your use of Wordstar, Lotus 1-2-3
and dBase II, since I am familiar with all three of these packages.
I am confident I could not only run your existing systems, but also
expand the uses of the computer in the Real Estate business.

Thank you for considering me for the position of Computer Assistant
at Leisure Realty.

I look forward to hearing from you.

Sincerely,

John Villiers

John Villiers

Winning Interview Techniques

The interview has been set up. Finally the efforts of your job campaign have come to fruition—you have been granted an interview. You know the time, the place, the importance of doing well. Suddenly you have an attack of nerves. You're both eager and anxious.

How will it go? Will you be able to convince the interviewer that not only can you do the job, but, indeed, you are absolutely the best person for it? You feel a little insecure. Will you be able to articulate your qualifications adequately?

What is happening to you happens to almost every job hunter: You're having a slight case of interview jitters. Don't worry; you're in good company. No matter how high up one is on the corporate ladder, being placed in the proverbial "hot seat" can be an unsettling experience. Our experience, as well as that of our colleagues all over the country, confirms that the great majority of job seekers find the interview the most stressful part of job hunting.

There are ways, however, of lessening that stress. The first step is to view the interview realistically. In most cases, job candidates tend to view the interview as an acid test of their abilities and self-worth. Such an attitude is extremely anxiety producing, and is guaranteed to elicit a negative response from the interviewer. But viewed realistically, the interview is simply a meeting between two equals—a buyer and a seller—to explore what each has to offer. Always keep in mind that feeling of equality between you and the interviewer.

The person conducting the interview is also under pressure. The interviewer must have the judgment to choose the most qualified candidate and must at the same time generate enough enthusiasm about the employer that when an offer is made, it will be accepted. Just as you are in competition with many other applicants, companies recruiting employees are similarly in competition with other employers trying to hire just the right person.

You were asked to be interviewed because some person in the company—an executive, an officer, the personnel director, or another representative of the employer—felt that the company's best interests would be served by knowing more about you. Your résumé generated interest in you. It indicated to them that you are qualified; now they are trying to determine if you are the *best* qualified.

With this in mind, you must now convince them that it is in their best interests to hire you. You must present yourself in such a manner that your assets and abilities are superior to any other candidate.

We are not surprised to find that the job does not always go to the most qualified person. It is possible to predict with a high degree of reliability which candidates will receive not one, but many job offers. We have analyzed the common denominator, the quality that these winners possess. It is that they give a first impression that projects honesty, sincerity, and enthusiasm. Given several candidates with virtually identical credentials, the job will almost invariably go to the individual projecting the most positive and enthusiastic image.

Creating The Right Impression

Because the very first impression you make will carry through the entire interview and greatly determine its outcome, it is of vital importance to create the most positive image possible. Your physical appearance, mannerisms, vocabulary, attitude, and nonverbal communication all contribute to the impression you make.

How do you convey the impression of sincerity? By being honest, open, and real. Simply by being yourself. Assume the attitude that the company wants you, and feel confident; this starts the self-fulfilling prophesy. *Feel* successful and chances are you *will* be successful.

Any form of role-playing that projects a personality other than your own is bound to lead to a disastrous interview. There is no way to predict what kind of person the employer is looking for and, if in fact you know, it is highly unlikely you could keep up the performance for the duration of the interview. Likewise, don't try to second guess an interviewer and tell him or her what you think they want to hear. It will almost always backfire.

Doing Your Homework

Because the interview is such a crucial part of the hiring process, take time to prepare yourself. This preparation will add to your self-confidence.

Your résumé will form the basis of the interview. No doubt, the interviewer will want you to elaborate upon some of the items you have mentioned only briefly. It is imperative that you review the résumé carefully before the interview. In fact, it is advisable to spend some time going over documentation, status reports, performance reviews, flow diagrams, or whatever you can in order to refresh your memory about previous projects or systems cited in the résumé. This will enable you to give specific technical details about your previous work, and demonstrate your thorough understanding of the system.

Many managers use the interview, not only as a way of evaluating a candidate, but also to enhance their own technical background. After all, here you are, telling the interviewer that you've had experience with System X, possibly one that the interviewer always wanted to know about. Just be sure you don't give wrong answers or guess at the answers to questions you're not sure of. You can never tell when the interviewer may, in fact, be a world class expert on just the type of system he or she is naively asking you to explain. If you don't know the answer to a technical question, just say so!

Managers become very suspicious if they ask for a technical explanation and get an evasive answer filled with generalities. Be sure to describe in detail any system design or coding techniques you may have created or used which illustrates your particular contribution.

If you are seeking a job with a hardware or software vendor, find out as much as possible about the products. A good way to do this is by writing to the marketing and sales organization asking for information, or by studying the description of the product in reference materials put out by publications such as *Datapro* or *Data Decisions.*

If you are seeking a management position, it will be valuable for you to learn as much as possible about the company conducting the interview. Find out whether it is a public or privately owned corporation. If listed on one of the major stock exchanges, find out how the stock is doing. Your broker may be able to give you insights into the history of the company.

In short, know the basic facts. The names of officers or partners, number of employees, and so on. Your local library is a source of such information. Directories such as *Standard & Poors, Dun & Bradstreet,* and *Moody's* will also be extremely useful. The business periodical index will help you locate any recent press coverage. Spend some time reading current and back issues of trade journals that deal with the computer industry. It is possible you may come across an article referring to one of the companies that have invited you for an interview. Appearing up to date is an excellent method of scoring points.

Further Preparation

Make sure you organize your thoughts in advance to answer some of the tough questions which almost certainly come up during the interview process.

If you are between jobs, your reasons for leaving the last one will undoubtedly be probed during the interview. If presently employed, you will be asked the reasons you are seeking a new position. Preparing for these questions will provide you with the confidence you need to do your best. Always answer every question honestly. If you were fired, tell the simple truth. In these times of retrenchment, mergers, relocations, and layoffs, firing has become as familiar as television. Chances are that your prospective boss is no stranger to the experience, and will find it easy to empathize with you if you deal with the situation honestly.

If you were fired because your performance was in question, answer truthfully and try to transmit the extent to which you made this a learning experience. Never make any negative comments about a former staff member or your former or present employer.

More than likely you will be asked why you want to work for the company you are visiting. Again, be brief. Be also exact and direct. The research you have done about that particular employer will help you point out why you feel good about the interviewing company and how you can make a positive contribution to it. Wanting to move up, to earn a higher salary, to join a larger (or smaller) organization, having a desire to relocate; or wanting to make a career change—all these are appropriate reasons for looking for a new job. To sum it up, be as honest on your interview as you were on your résumé.

Asking Questions is Important, Too

Interviewers frequently pay as much attention to the questions candidates ask as to the answers they give. The questions you ask will serve as an indication of how much you have understood of what the interviewer had told you, and will show your level of competence and sophistication. Listen carefully and ask intelligent questions about the system, program, machine, or application that you will be working on. After all, you are also basing a decision about this job and this company on what you learn at the interview. Turn the interview into a true meeting of equals by politely, but firmly, asking the questions which are important to you.

Some of the questions you probably want to ask are:

☐ What system/program/machine/application, etc., will you be working on?

☐ What role will you play? Maintenance? Support? Development? Management?

☐ Will you be part of a team, and if so how big? Or will you be working alone?

☐ What is the current state of development on the system, and what problems are anticipated?

☐ What software tools are available?

☐ Are computer time and access readily available?

☐ Are there any benefits such as home terminals, personal computer purchase plans, bonuses, or stock options?

Though every interview is different, all will include questions requiring more than a "yes" or "no" answer. The interviewer will be listening not only for content, but for sincerity, poise, judgment, and ability to think quickly.

Spend some time before the interview developing answers to the following questions that you think might give you trouble. With a friend, husband, or wife—or even a tape recorder—go through each question. Prepare answers to give extemporaneously. There are no right or wrong answers. The purpose is to find out more about the subjective you. Aim for clarity, brevity, and, above all, honesty. Remember also that the actual wording and substance of these questions will vary to reflect the circumstances of each particular interview.

You will find two sets of questions. The first are questions geared specifically for programmers. If you are looking for a job in some other aspect of the computer industry, they may not all be relevant, but are worth reviewing in any event.

The second set is more general. These questions tend to be asked regardless of the specific job you are seeking, and you should be prepared to answer them.

Programming-Related Questions

1. What is the most technically difficult problem you've had to solve? Describe your solution.
2. What program/system etc., that you have written are you most proud of and why?
3. What is your best programming language?
4. How would you rank yourself as a programmer?
5. Do you subscribe to a particular programming methodology and why?
6. Which hardware/operating system/database/programming language/tp monitor/etc., do you prefer and why?
7. Do you own a home computer? If so, what do you use it for?
8. Do you prefer doing maintenance, development, or support? Why?
9. How do you document your code?
10. How do you test the code you've written?
11. How do you prevent the introduction of bugs into systems you've worked on?
12. What do you like about programming? What do you dislike?
13. What current trend in the computer industry do you think will have the greatest effect on your career?
14. What computer-related course was most valuable to you and why?
15. Compare and contrast two specific languages/systems/ databases/machines/etc., that you've worked on giving the strengths and weaknesses of each.

16. Describe the worst or most difficult system/program/application/database/etc., that you have worked on. What made it difficult?
17. What are the most important functions of an operating system/database/compiler/tp monitor/etc.?
18. Do you prefer interacting with users or customers; or simply working alone on your terminal?
19. Describe the data structure of a filing system or database you have worked on.
20. Compare the design and functionality of a microcomputer with that of a mainframe.

General Questions

1. What do you consider to be your strong points?
2. What do you consider to be your weak points?
3. What motivates you?
4. What is your definition of success?
5. What did you enjoy most about your last job?
6. What did you like least about your last position?
7. Where would you like your career to be in five years?
8. What are your short-term career goals?
9. Do you prefer to work alone, or as part of a team?
10. How do you get along with your peers?
11. How good are you in motivating people?
12. To what magazines do you subscribe?
13. What newspapers do you read?
14. What were the last three books you read?
15. What are your hobbies?
16. How do you spend your leisure time?
17. Are you active in community affairs? If so, describe.
18. Why do you want to change jobs?
19. Why are you unemployed?
20. Why do you think you would be an asset to the company?
21. How well do you work under pressure?
22. How do you feel about working overtime?
23. Would you be willing to relocate to one of our branch offices?
24. How do you feel about working for a woman (man) or younger person?
25. What did you learn in your last position?
26. How did you get along with your boss on your last job?
27. How did you get along with the staff in your last job?
28. Why do you want to work for this company?
29. What do you consider your outstanding achievements?
30. What kinds of problems do you enjoy solving?
31. How often have you been ill in the past five years?
32. Are you willing to take a physical exam?
33. Are you willing to take a series of personality (aptitude) tests?

34. Would you be willing to take a lie detector test?
35. Do you have government clearance?
36. Have you ever applied for clearance and been turned down? If yes, why?
37. Have you ever been fired? If yes, why?
38. Do you have management ability? Describe?
39. How ambitious are you?
40. What was your last salary? What is your minimum salary at this time?

Salary Negotiation

It is the policy of most companies to conduct a series of interviews, because the employer is interested in the opinions of several members of the staff. This, of course, works both ways. It allows the applicant to learn more about the company—to decide if a rapport can be established with members of the firm and get first-hand knowledge of working conditions in that particular company. In general, the more interviews you are invited to, the more seriously you are being considered.

Treat each individual interview with the same serious approach as the first. Always be prompt. It's a good idea to schedule no more than two interviews a day: one in the morning and another in the afternoon, since there is no way of telling how long an interview will last. Be a good listener, but feel free to ask any question that will be relevant.

Usually the question of salary will come up at the final or near final interview. Never begin salary negotiations until you are quite certain you have a job offer. In fact, don't bring up the subject of compensation; let the potential employer take the first step.

When asked about your present or last compensation package, answer concisely, including all bonuses and benefits. If you feel you were underpaid, mention that as one of the reasons for wanting to change jobs.

If you were referred to the employer by an employment agency or headhunter, it's a good idea to let them do the negotiating for you. Since they are very aware of market conditions and, in effect, will profit by your being hired, they will attack the question of compensation very vigorously. Their fee is usually based on a percentage of your salary, so it is in their best interest, as well as yours, to get the highest possible salary. Besides, as mentioned before, it's always helpful to have a third party negotiate for you.

If you are forced to do your own negotiating, stay flexible. If you know what salary range is being offered, put your salary expectations at the high end of the range. Remember, the interview is a screening process; if your requested minimum salary is considerably higher than the employer tends to pay, this could knock you out of the running.

Don't get boxed into a specific figure before you have to. Always talk in $5,000 to $10,000 ranges. If the interview has gone well and you are really interested in the company, aim high and then negotiate. Be sure to get all the relevant information concerning benefits: medical and dental insurance, profit-sharing plans, future salary increases, stock options, and so on. Consider all of the above as part of the total salary. If the subject of salary hasn't yet come up, and you are asked about your salary expectations, one approach is to answer the question with one of your own, "I'm glad you brought up the subject of compensation. What is the salary range for this job?" Give the employer a chance to give a figure, and then negotiate from there.

It's a good idea never to make a decision at the interview—whether it's the first, second and/or third interview. Ask for a few days or a week to think it over.

Thank the employer for the offer and indicate that you will give it serious consideration. Let them know when you will call back with your answer—no longer than a week or two. Bear in mind that the company will continue interviewing until the job has been filled, so don't delay too long. Give yourself just enough time to weigh any other offers and reflect more thoroughly on this one.

Sample Résumés

On the following pages you'll see a great many sample résumés. One of them may appeal to you as an example to follow. Even though parts of the samples, especially the job descriptions, may resemble what you wish to express, never copy them verbatim. These samples are included only to give you ideas that you can use to write your own résumé.

Use your completed worksheets, along with the form of the résumé you decide to use, and start writing. You will probably have to re-write several times before you are completely satisfied with the results. Don't get discouraged!

Be sure to include all the pertinent information, and adhere to basic rules governing presentation and content. Here are some of those rules, the do's and don'ts of writing a job-getting résumé.

1. DO keep it brief.
2. DO place your name, address, and phone number in a conspicuous place.
3. DO include all degrees, colleges or universities attended, and dates you received degrees.
4. DO list present job first, continuing in reverse chronological order.
5. DO list all dates of employment, leaving no unexplained gaps.
6. DO include all information regarding familiarity with hardware, software, and computer languages.
7. DO use plenty of white space.
8. DO be sure your résumé is easy to read.
9. DO use 1 or 2 sheets of 8½ × 11-inch paper, preferably white bond.
10. DO be sure there are no misspellings; proofread carefully.
11. DO NOT make your résumé too long.
12. DO NOT include long, hard-to-read paragraphs.
13. DO NOT use fancy binders, mixed type faces, colored papers.
14. DO NOT include height, weight, age, sex, marital status, or number of children.
15. DO NOT include salary requirements or past salaries.

COMPUTER OPERATIONS

NAME   Lisa R. Cosack

ADDRESS 987 Chicago Street
         St. Louis, Missouri 63101
         (314) 548-4375

OBJECTIVE   Senior Operator in Progressive Computer Installation

EXPERIENCE

1982 to
present

AVCO DATA SERVICES, St. Louis, Missouri
Operate, monitor, and control electronic
computers and associated peripheral equipment required to do batch processing on a
wide variety of business applications in
a real-time, on-line environment via disk
or tape. Equipment used is DIGITAL KL, KI,
PDP-10 computers. Also responsible for
monitoring, dumping, and loading the associated communication equipment, PDP-11/34 and
PDP-11/40. Responsible for backing up customer files and servicing them as needed.

1972 to
1982

INTERACTIVE SYSTEMS CORPORATION, Kansas City, Kansas
Duties included operating and monitoring
controlling 3 UNIVAC/494 and a DIGITAL KL PDP-
10, in a real-time, on-line processing environment and their associated peripheral equipment.
Responsible for the file transfer of customers'
files and other related in-house duties.

1973 to
1977

KANSAS TRUST COMPANY, Kansas City, Missouri
Duties included operating and monitoring
an IBM 370/135 computer and its associated
peripheral equipment for an in-house environment. Responsibilities were updating checking
and savings accounts which were transacted during the day and worked with payroll, school
scheduling, and tax billing.

EDUCATION

St. Paul's Jr. College
    Associate in Science Degree in Computer Science;
    Graduated June, 1980; courses in COBOL, Fortran,
    RPG, JCL, System Design, and Digital Electronics.

Electronic Computer Programming Institute
    Certificate in Computer Programming in COBOL,
    RPG, BAL; graduated June 1973.

IBM-DATA CENTER
    Operating Course in DOS/VS using Power.

Kirkland High School
    College Preparatory Program; Graduated 1972.

References upon request

RÉSUMÉ OF LAURIE ADAMS

ADDRESS
24 Oak Park Road
Peekskill, New York 11304
(914) 341-4416

EDUCATION
1981
to
Present
MEREDITH COLLEGE, Yorktown Heights, New York
Candidate for a Bachelor of Science degree in
Computer Information Systems.

1982
PRIME COMPUTER, INC., Framingham, Massachusetts
Attended Prime Customer Education session in Computer
Operations.

1981
DIGITAL EQUIPMENT CORPORATION, Bedford, Massachusetts
Attended Digital Customer Education session in Compu-
ter Operations.

HARDWARE/
SOFTWARE

DECsystem 1060	TOPS - 10
PRIME 850, 750	Primos/ Information
SYCOR 405	

PROFESSIONAL
EXPERIENCE
BAINBRIDGE MANUFACTURING, Yorktown Heights, New York

1981
to
Present
Computer Operator

Duties include operation of DEC 1060 and PRIME 850
computer system; resolving computer control messages
when required; independently managing operator's
functions, such as loading tapes, cards, disk packs,
and paper; perform system backups and user retrievals;
monitor and control user job traffic.

1979
to
1981
SKLAR SYSTEMS, Peekskill, New York

Production Control Assistant

Responsible for manufacturing production control in-
cluding material control, production scheduling, WIP
inventory records, planning, and expediting.

* Project Assistant on MRP Project: Implemented
and maintained MRP System, including Item
Master File, control data, and transaction data.

Purchasing/Production Control Secretary

Handled complete range of secretarial duties.

* Promoted to Production Control Assistant

REFERENCES
Furnished upon request.

MILLARD POLLACK
1428 Cornelia Street
Brooklyn, N.Y. 11227
(212) EV 4-3366

Position Objective

Lead Operator or Shift Supervisor with a progressive organization that
will make full use of my education and experience, my knowledge of systems,
and my ability to direct and supervise.

Work Experience

SYSTEMS OPERATOR   7/82 to Present
Andersen International, New York
(Designers of a software management information system for the cable industry)

* Responsible for ensuring the efficient operation of the VAX/VMS
  11/750 system, by knowing the needs of the users of the system
  in accordance with the capabilities and limitations of VAX/VMS.

* Responsible for the daily, weekly, and other periodic operational
  procedures such as routine backup and restore procedures.

* Duties have included participation in technical support for clients
  for both the hardware and software; working with the systems manager
  in providing installations to new customers; and keeping track
  of service and software contracts with vendors.

SYSTEMS MANAGER   6/81 to 7/82
Great Neck Mental Health Center, Great Neck, New York

* Developed and implemented a complete MIS system. Managed conversion
  of an off-line environment to an on-line, real-time environment,
  and responsible for the installation of a PDP 11/24.

* Have knowledge of and experience with software packages, including
  testing, debugging, maintenance, system enhancements, and new
  program applications for Health Center practices.

* Supervised a technical staff, including hiring of personnel, problem
  solving, and interface with vendors.

SENIOR COMPUTER OPERATOR   1978 to 1981
Kenyon and Eckhardt Company, Baldwin, New York

* Responsibilities included scheduling and monitoring of EDP production,
  knowledge of IBM System 3, and exposure to programming RPG II.

Millard Pollack, page 2

Education

Digital Training Center
Bedford, Massachusetts; 1982.   VAX/VMS System Operators Course.

Commonwealth College
New York City; 1978.   Data Processing, Basic Language.

Queens College
New York City; 1976 to 1978.   B.A. Degree, Magna Cum Laude.

References

        Available upon request.

BERNARD LENAPE

135-31 112th Street   South Ozone Park, NY 11420   (212) 529-8203

OBJECTIVE: <u>SENIOR COMPUTER OPERATOR</u>

HARDWARE: IBM 360/30   RCA SPECTRA 70/35
BURROUGHS B3500 and 4800   HONEYWELL 100 Series

OTHER SKILLS: Keypunch, Unit Record Equipment, Adding Machine,
Manual and Electric Typewriter, Record-Keeping

EDUCATION: Elizabeth Seton College, Yonkers, NY
1980-AAS, Business Administration

Borough of Manhattan Community College, New York, NY
1971-73-Liberal Arts/Data Processing

Northeast Region Education Center, New York, NY
1970-RCA Computer Systems Certificate in TOS/TDOS

Institute of Computer Technology, New York, NY
1969-Certificate in IBM Punched Card Data Processing
1964-Certificate in ABM Keypunch and IBM Keypunch

EXPERIENCE:

1977 to   BOWERY SAVINGS BANK, New York, NY
Present   <u>Computer Operator</u>

* Run bank applications on daily cycle; create
  tape and turnover log sheet. Use online
  thrift system (B4800).

* Debug COBOL programs: Compile, test and execute
  (if program has bug, take memory dump and send
  back to programming).

* Fill in as lead operator during vacations and
  absences.

1972-1977   AMERICAN INSTITUTE OF CERTIFIED PUBLIC ACCOUNTANTS,
New York, NY
<u>Lead Computer Operator</u> (1975-1977)
<u>Computer Operator</u> (1972-1975)

* Used B3500 online accounting system: Updated
  membership records, including names and
  addresses; maintained records on publications;
  ran all accounting applications.

* Balanced reports (located errors when reports
  were out of balance); debugged COBOL, RPG, and
  FORTRAN programs.

1972   SOCIETY OF AUTOMOTIVE ENGINEERS, New York, NY
               Computer Operator

               * Ran entire computer operation on IBM 360/30;
                  designed in-house job request forms.

1969-1972   BOROUGH OF MANHATTAN COMMUNITY COLLEGE, New York, NY
               Computer Operator

               * Trained students in operation of IBM 360/30,
                  RCA SPECTRA 70/35, and keypunch machines; super-
                  vised student aides; tutored students in COBOL
                  programming (BASIC) in basic and advanced appli-
                  cations; evaluated performance.

               * Compiled and debugged COBOL, ALP, RPG, BAL pro-
                  grams for administration and students; maintained
                  tape library.

               * Given opportunity to experiment with system to
                  determine extent of applications available.

REFERENCES: On request.

Nancy Jones
47 Main Street
Des Moines, Iowa 50321
(515) 270-9431

Hardware: IBM 3081, 3033, 3032, 4341, 370/168, System 34,
                        Xerox 9700, VAX 11/780, REGITEL, ENTREX

Software: OS/MVS, JES 2, VM/CMS, DOS/VS, IDMS, CICS, TLMS,
                        DYNAM IT, UCC7 & 11, PANVALET, MARK IV, TOTAL,
                        TOP SECRET, IBM/JCL

Work
Experience: FARMER'S INSURANCE & LOAN CO., Des Moines, Iowa
                        Production Control Manager

3/82 - present   Established a computer production control
                        department. Scheduled, processed, verified,
                        and distributed all major batch systems.
                        Supervised a staff of 13 on 3 shifts.
                        Major accomplishments included:
                        *Implementing a new customer billing system
                        *Defining control procedures
                        *Defining MVS JCL standards
                        *Assisting in the design of new forms
                        *Establishing micro-form needs to satisfy
                         user, programming, audit, and security
                         requirements

1/81 - 3/82   TRAVELER'S MANUFACTURING GROUP, Omaha, Nebraska
                        Senior Production Control Analyst

                        Assisted the production control manager to
                        establish this new department. Specific
                        projects included:
                        *Writing operational documentation for new
                         systems (both batch and on-line)
                        *Controlling the conversion from impact to
                         laser (3800) printing with minimal effect
                         on users
                        *Establishing standards for data and computer
                         control procedures

1975-1981   STATE OF NEBRASKA, Omaha, Nebraska
                        Senior Data Controller

                        Controlled computer-based systems for a variety
                        of applications. Coordinated with user depart-
                        ments for both data input and output reports,
                        as well as with scheduling and operations per-
                        sonnel for mainframe (IBM-370/158) and mini-
                        computer (General Automation) processing

Maintained and updated relevant documentation
for each system as it affected data control,
operations, and the user departments. Provided
verification of the accuracy of output reports
(detailed financial procedures were commonly involved). Considerable exposure to, and some detailed involvement with:
  *DOS/VS operating systems and associated JCL;
   PANVALET from Pansophic Systems to maintain
   source libraries and core image libraries;
   DYNAM/T from Computer Associates to maintain
   magnetic media records; CICS/VS (IBM) on-line
   systems; MARK IV from Informatics, a report
   generator; and TOTAL, a CINCOM database
   package.

1972 - 1975   KEANE ASSOCIATES, Chicago, Illinois
                  Operations Consultant

                  Intensively engaged in operation of a wide
                  variety of hardware, software assistance, and
                  operations systems work.
                    *Hands-on experience with on-line and off-line
                     terminals, including Rank, Honeywell, IBM
                     (360-370), NCR, and ICL equipment

1968 - 1972   Shift Leader/Operator - Various Companies.

References upon request.

Joan Jumont
220-B South Beron Street
Byron, Pa. 16917

(814) 909-3516

OBJECTIVE: A challenging, growth-oriented position as Production
Control Supervisor in which comprehensive education, hands-on
training and experience, and analytical ability would
be of value.

EDUCATION:
1983-present

Lafayette College   Easton, Pennsylvania
Major Studies: Computer Science

1980-1982

Lehigh College   Easton, Pennsylvania
Major Studies: Data Processing/Math and General Education
(1977-1980)

1979-1980

Stroudsburg Institute of Technology Stroudsburg, Pennsylvania
Major Studies: Computer Programming/Math Sciences

SUMMARY: Over 4 years Computer Operator: Entry and Verification
experience. Excellent communication skills both verbal
and written. Data Processing experience involves ability
to modify/change/update data; transfer data for duplication
and verifications. Supervision and Training/Employee
Scheduling. Ability to complete projects under stressful
conditions.

**WORK
HISTORY:**

Air Express   Byron, Pennsylvania
DISPATCHER/COMPUTER OPERATOR

1977-present

Began employment as Data Control Clerk and gained four
years experience. Handled extensive data entries/verifications;
processed reports and related documents; monitored data
entries for irregularities and made appropriate corrections.
In addition, became experienced and adept with data duplication transfers performed in daily activity.

Promoted after proven ability to Dispatcher in 1981. Responsible for employee work scheduling; monitored deliveries/
return trips and consistently improved working schedules/
productivity in this regard. Supervised/trained and issued
scheduling to over 150+ drivers; handled claims reports/follow-
up including damages/returns; truck breakdowns and emergency
repair services/preventative maintenance. Advised management on improvements in customer services and scheduling that
enhanced over-all operations.

**SPECIAL
STRENGTHS:**

Strongly enjoy chosen field of endeavor. Dependable, honest and
growth-minded employee. Enjoy working with people; work
exceptionally well with co-workers and management. Capable
manager who brings positive business personality, hands-on
programming training/education, and analytical-minded abilities
to new business environments. Willing to work long hours to
complete projects and ensure smooth-running operations.

REFERENCES: Professional references furnished upon request
                 Willing to travel/relocate
                 Salary negotiable

EVELYN PLUMER
259 Ridge Lane
Danbury, Connecticut 06810
203-742-3301

OBJECTIVE: Telecommunications Manager, Voice and Data
Networks.

EXPERTISE: IBM/SNA, ACF/NCP Multisystem Networking, VTAM,
DEC, Honeywell, H-P, Voice & Data, Personal
Computers, Packet Switch Networking, Network
Switching Systems. Satellite, UHF/VHF Radio,
Microwave & Telephony experience with USAF sup-
porting World-Wide Voice & Data Communications
Systems.

EDUCATION: M.B.A. 1976
Brown University, Providence, R.I.

B.A. Management 1971
Barnard College, New York City

EXPERIENCE: ITT, Danbury, Connecticut
1980 to
Present   Manager, Network Services   (1981 to present)
Manage the implementation and operation of all
corporate data communication networks which provide international service to over 1000 remote
terminals and personal computers. Optimized
network availability and performance of all network resources. Defined requirements and evaluated all new network services and products which
supported IBM/SNA, Honeywell, HP, and DEC computing services. Participated in strategic network planning and special studies to enhance
network utility, and implemented new services
such as Packet Switching and Networking of personal computers.

Telecommunications Operations Manager (1979 - 1980)
Implemented centralized control and operation of
corporation's private line voice network which
provided integrated voice and data services to
over 300 company locations. Managed the operational cutover to new Northern Telecom and Rolm
network switching systems. Implemented and
managed customized network control centers for
both voice and data network operations which
dramatically reduced problem resolution time.
Devised a centralized problem management and
help desk function to assist voice and data network end users.

1973 to 1980   RCA Corporation

                                Communications Technician
                                Held numerous engineering, maintenance,
                                and operational assignments supporting
                                world-wide voice and data communications
                                systems including MICROWAVE, SATELLITE,
                                VHF and UHF RADIO, and TELEPHONE (both
                                outside and inside plant).

References upon request

Willing to relocate

Résumé

Richard J. Lazarus
12 Roadside Avenue
Beechwood, Ohio   45208
(513) 862-1783

Employment Objective

To expand my career as an inhouse computer technician with the objective
of eventually moving toward an Engineering position

Education Background

Case Western University--Cleveland, Ohio

September 1977 December 1979	Engineering Technology Applied Technical Mathematics I & II, Calculus I and Physics I & II
September 1975	Control Data Institute subject area: Basic Electronics, Passive and Active, AC/DC, Solid State Theory, Digital, Microprocessors, Peripheral Equipment such as card readers, punches, line printers, tape drives, and all associated controllers, Central processing, hardware and software, machine language programming
September 1966 May 1970	Beechwood High School

Employment Experience

June 1980 - March 1984	LAMBDA CORPORATION INC., Beechwood, Ohio Senior Systems Test Technician, Group Leader Performed diverse technical duties in the testing and maintaining of sophisticated high-speed memories for large-scale IBM mainframe computers. Responsible for the system testing of all add-on products. Assisted in testing and development of additional storage on IBM's 370 Line, 158, 168, 3031, 3032, and 3033 computers. Exposed to extensive research and development of a new IBM 3081 compatible memory product and was instru- mental in initiating testing requirements for a viable product line.
April 1976 - August 1978	Production Test Technician Job consisted of frequent use of Teradyne diagnostic test equipment, point-to-point plexus setup, universal impedance testing, and pattern generator testing to component level. Performed daily testing on all related

sub-assemblies such as: mini cages, power supply setups, relay boxes, and any switch assembly associated with the product lines. Duties included working with oscilloscopes, DVM and Simpson Meters, reading schematics, manuals, and engineering sketches and following verbal instructions.

February 1973 –   CAPITOL STORES INC.
June 1976

Computer Operations

Position included processing of daily production jobs such as inventory control reports, perishable meat and produce billings, general ledger, accounts receivable, and accounts payable jobs. Complete training on an IBM 370-135, 138 DOS System.

References   References provided upon request.

Peter E. Bazarcus
132 Centre Street
Loris, S.C. 29569
(803) 661-2490

OBJECTIVE

Employment as a computer technician that will offer me a wide range of experience in the computer field. The opportunity to advance is a prime objective.

EDUCATIONAL BACKGROUND

9/1979 - Present   TDR Institute of Technology - Electronic Technology (Evening Program)

3/1978 - 6/1979   Columbia College (S.C.) - Computer Science (Evening Program)

9/1970 - 6/1971   South Carolina Community College - Business Management and Accounting

9/1968 - 5/1970   Loris High School - Graduate in college preparatory curriculum

EMPLOYMENT EXPERIENCE

2/1977-Present   SWAB, BURK & SHULMAN   Myrtle Beach, SC

Computer Terminal Technician

Trouble-shoot and repair terminals and communication equipment. Wire terminals to the computer, install and maintain data communication lines for our local Network, set up and test terminals prior to accepting, keep inventory, order and return spare parts.
*Contact person for various manufacturers; schedule repair work and handle user complaints.
*Types of terminals worked on: DEC VT-100, VT-52, LA-120 and LA-36; Texas Instruments 720 725, 730, 733, 735, 743 and 745; H.D.S. Concept-100; and Teleray 3711.
*Communication equipment: Racal-Vadic 3467 modems; Codex LSI 9600 modem and Codex 6010 multiplexer.

Computer Technician Trainee (2/1977-6/1979)

Maintained Data Product 2550 charaband line printers. Ran diagnostic tests on D.E.C. KL-10 and KA-10 systems. Performed preventive maintenance on DEC/Memorex RPO-6 disk drives and Calcomp 230 disk drives, ran test on drives using exerciser and replaced or aligned printheads.

| 12/1975-2/1977 | PRUDENTIAL INSURANCE COMPANY | Myrtle Beach, SC |

Computer and Microfiche Operator

Console operator, monitor system; reloaded the system (Univac 1108, 1110), changed disk packs, mounted tapes, reset terminal lines, dealt with users and output breakdown. Used a mini-computer to transfer data from tape to microfiche, performed preventive maintenance on microfiche equipment, mixed the chemicals for developing the microfiche, and distributed the finished microfiche.

| 1972-1975 | SEAFOOD ISLAND RESTAURANT | Loris, SC |

Owner/Proprietor

In charge of personnel, bookkeeping, and dealing with customers.

OTHER EDUCATION

Heathkit Electronics - basic DC and AC electronic individual study courses.

Digital Equipment Corporation - Introduction to digital computer logic.

Swab, Burk & Shulman - Bitgraph maintenance.

ACHIEVEMENTS

At Swab, Burk & Shulman, I initiated a quicker method of getting faster turnaround time from outside vendors and implementation of an on-line inventory system of spare parts.

INTERESTS

auto mechanics, tennis, jogging, softball, and fishing.

REFERENCES

References will be furnished upon request.

JAMES E. VANDERBILT III
273 RIVER STREET
BAKERSFIELD, CA
93309
(209) 556-2590

EXPERIENCE

5/81-8/84   ROCK CREEK CORPORATION, Modesto, Ca.

Position: Computer Technician II
Responsible for the maintenance and set-up of
all in-house Digital Equipment Corporation
equipment to user and client specifications,
including troubleshooting and repair, upgrading,
and reconfiguration of model systems. Additional responsibilities included: assisting in the
design of hardware prototypes; effective communication and interaction with DEC field service department; updating and re-writing company policies
and procedures; development and maintenance of
technical files; and customer assistance through
telephone diagnostics and occasional field service.

2/79-4/81   JARBER DIVISION OF DALTON SCIENTIFIC, Bakersfield, Ca.

Position: Computer Technician
Responsibilities included the set-up and configuration of Digital Equipment Corporation systems to
Jarber specifications; confirmation of proper initial
power-up; troubleshooting faulty units to the component level; and running RT-11 and RSX-11 DEC
diagnostics.

7/78-11/79   TERCHIL INCORPORATED, Modesto, Ca.

Position: Electronic Technician
Responsibilities included troubleshooting and re-
pairing modems and various telecommunications
equipment to the component level.

EDUCATION AND TRAINING

October 1980   DIGITAL FINANCE, INC., Bakersfield, Ca.

Received a certificate for successfully completing
PDP 11/23 Hardware and Interfacing course.

2/77-9/77   TECHNOLOGY INSTITUTE, Modesto, Ca.

Received a certificate in Computer Electronics in
October 1979. Completed advancement courses in
BASIC and microprocessors.

REFERENCES   Will be furnished upon request.

PROGRAMMERS

Bob McGlavflin
2012 Baker Street
Chicago, Illinois 60698
(312) 598-7240

OBJECTIVE

A suitable position in programming, software development, or technical support

SOFTWARE/HARDWARE

Pascal, Basic, CDC Mix Assembler, GPSS, Cobol, familiarity with APL, LISP and SNOBOL 4

Operating systems - CP/M, CDC NOS, TRS DOS

CDC Cyber 6000; Sanyo MBC-1000, TRS 80 and Tl 99-4A micro-computers

EDUCATION

University of Chicago
    B.S. in Computer Science with Math minor to be awarded
    May 1984
    Currently completing nontechnical course requirement
    Computer Science Courses included Operating Systems and
    Computer Architecture, Data Structures, Discrete Structures,
    and Programming Languages

SOFTWARE EXPERIENCE

SPIRO MISSILES, Chicago, Illinois, 10/83 - Present

Programmer

In Sanyo MBC-1000 microcomputer under CP/M using Basic, responsibilities include software implemention and user training.

MCI/UNIVERSITY OF CHICAGO, Fall 1983

Computer Instructor

Taught computer fundamentals and BASIC language using TRS 80 to inmates of correctional institution.

UNIVERSITY OF CHICAGO COMPUTER SERVICES, 9/80 - 12/81

Instructor Taught introductory computer courses to students and faculty members; co-wrote user manuals for CDC Cyber 6000 System Commands and Text Editor.

<u>Computer Operator</u> of CDC Cyber 6000. Responsible for running student, faculty, and administrative batch jobs and routing output to departments.

<u>Lab Monitor</u> Maintained CRT and DECwriter systems; answered student questions regarding system problems; wrote documentation for APL and CDC Text Editor.

<u>REFERENCES</u>

Available upon request.

Paul F. Roderigo   Telephone: (918) 621-4101
72 Cornell Avenue
Tulsa, Oklahoma 74105

OBJECTIVE: Entry-level position in computer programming.

EDUCATION: ALPHA COMPUTER INSTITUTE, Tulsa, Oklahoma
10/82-3/83
                  Graduated from the 653-hour Computer/Programming/Operations
                  curriculum, 130 hours ahead of schedule. Wrote, tested,
                  and debugged 18 programs:
                  Languages: COBOL, FORTRAN, RPGII, BASIC
                  Procedures: Included input data validation, sorting, record
                                 updating, use of arrays, looping, indexing,
                                 subroutines, decimal and binary calculations.
                  Applications: Included data base updates, accounting
                                 routines, brokerage reports.
                  Processing: Disk, punched cards, printed reports.

                  Completed section on Business Systems Analysis and Design
                  and Accounting Principles.

                  TULSA STATE COLLEGE, Tulsa, Oklahoma
9/77-5/82
                  Graduated from 5-year Cooperative Education Program with
                  a Bachelor of Science Degree in Criminal Justice.

                  JOHN JAY COLLEGE OF CRIMINAL JUSTICE, New York
9/76-5/77

EMPLOYMENT: THE WAVERLY CORPORATION, Tulsa, Oklahoma
1/81-present
                  Security Officer.
                  Provided access control of admittance of guests and employees
                  to insure security for the corporation. Performed a nightly
                  security sweep checking for open safes.

                  Participated in special security details at secret meetings
                  and seminars required by the corporation. Attained security
                  clearance level of secret as designated by the Department
                  of Defense.

                  TULSA AUXILIARY POLICE DEPARTMENT, Tulsa, Oklahoma
7/79-8/80
                  Auxiliary Police Officer.
                  Sworn in as an officer with police powers. Insured safety
                  of citizens by successfully handling social disturbances
                  to maintain community order.

Paul F. Roderigo
Page 2

TULSA POLICE DEPARTMENT, Tulsa, Oklahoma

2/79-5/79
5/78-11/78   Police Intern.
              Compiled and analyzed crime and accident statistics.
              Presented crime statistics to Chief of Police monthly.
              Coordinated movements of patrol officers as part of dispatcher
              duties. Participated in training with the day patrol officers.

REFERENCES: Will be furnished upon request.

HOWARD K. DONALDSON
1170 East Sycamore Lane
Nashville, Tennessee 37204
(615) LO-3-5341

EDUCATION:
  UNIVERSITY OF CHICAGO   B.S.
  Chicago, Illinois   1975   Social Welfare

TECHNICAL EDUCATION:
  OXFORD INSTITUTE FOR COMPUTER PROGRAMMING   1983
  Nashville, Tennessee   Certificate

  A six-month program of intensive software instruction equivalent to
  one year or more of entry-level professional experience, consisting
  of 450 hours of programming in 4 languages and more than 200 hours
  of studies in JCL, logic and design, systems analysis, business
  systems, database management, and data concepts. 350/400 hours on
  state-of-the-art hardware provided additional experience.

  Hardware: IBM 3081 OS/MVS (F.W. Faxon)
                   Editor: SPF under PANVALET/TSO

  Languages: COBOL, PL/1, ASSEMBLER, FORTRAN

  Techniques: Topdown structured design, control break processing,
                   sorts, table handling, data validation, flowcharting
                   and hierarchy charts, data dictionaries, sequential
                   and VSAM file updating, utilities, abend analysis,
                   storage dump interpretations.

PROFESSIONAL EXPERIENCE:
  Aetna Insurance Co.   Policy Examiner   1976-1982
  Nashville, Tennessee

  Audited and rated commercial and personal lines policies: kept
  informed of changes in state laws, rulings, and interpretations;
  critiqued client company policies and recommended changes; provided
  a smooth avenue of communication with client companies ensuring con-
  fidentiality of sensitive data; internal consultant of all changes
  in rulings and interpretations.

  Greenmount   Counselor   1973-1976
  Nashville, Tennessee

  Responsible for mentally and physically disabled clients in a halfway
  house; interviewed prospective residents; developed educational
  programs; arranged job placements; supervised household on weekends.

COMMENTS:

* Earned 9 quarter-hours of credit in COBOL programming on DEC VAX 11/780 using SOS editor at Tennessee University in 1981.

* Additional training in ASSEMBLER and BASIC at the Science Resource Center.

* Worked and financed 100% of college education.

* Work effectively in an individual or team effort.

Patricia Lowry
72 Wash St.
Skokie, Illinois 60077

(312) 651-3987

Job Objective: Programmer Trainee

Experience

1975-present   Global Electrical Technicians--Chicago, Illinois
                   Computer Operator

                   Operate and monitor digital computer equipment (3083).
                   Follow established programs and new programs under
                   development. Select appropriate processing devices
                   (card, tape, disc) and load computer. Observe lights
                   on console and storage devices to report deviations
                   from standards.

                   Maintain records of job performance; check and maintain
                   controls on each job. Solve operational problems and
                   check out new programs; assist in making necessary
                   corrections. Assist less experienced operators.

1972-1974   Tab Newspaper--Dundee, Illinois
                   Bookkeeper/Clerk Typist

                   Typed invoices; posted and maintained records and files;
                   made and verified computations. Typed classified ads
                   and sent to composing department.

Education   1971 B.A. degree from University of Chicago
                   Mathematics Major - Business studies and computer training
                   Activities - Advertising Manager of campus newspaper
                                Volunteer hospital work

References   Provided on request.

John Corwin
62 Pine Street
Scarsdale, New York 10583
(914) 823-1234

EDUCATION

May 1984

Fontbonne College
B.A., Mathematics - GPA: 3.94/4.0

In addition to the study of theoretical and applied
mathematics, concentration has been in the areas of
computer science and business. Courses include
FORTRAN, BASIC, COBOL, Systems Science, Operations
Research, Accounting, Economics and Investments.

EXPERIENCE

September 1981
to Present

Atlas Corporation
Larchmont, New York 10538

SCIENTIFIC PROGRAMMER/DATA BASE ANALYST
(Full Time May 1983 to August 1983 (CO-OP) -
Part Time 25-35 hours per week, August 1983 to Present)

Assigned to the Computer Aided Technology Project in
the Scientific Data Base Management Systems group.
Duties and responsibilities include:
- Participation in efficiency testing of Model
  204 Data Base Management System to be used
  in the Computer Aided Design Drafting system.
- Participation in the design of Back-Up and
  Recovery techniques and Security Features of
  the system.
- Design and initialization of Data Bases.
- Application User Support for Model 204 system.
- Teaching Data Base classes.

Application Programming was done in FORTRAN using TSO
on IBM 3033 MVS JES III systems.

(Same Organization)
SCIENTIFIC PROGRAMMER
(Full Time (CO-OP) - January 1983 to May 1983
                   - May 1982 to December 1982
                   - September 1981 to December 1981)

Duties and responsibilities included:
- Tape Management for Flight Simulation Labs.
- Graphical Analysis of simulated flight data.
- Programming in FORTRAN, MATLOC, and CSMP to
  analyze a digital control system for aircraft.
- Development of modeling programs to simulate
  the effectiveness of the control system on the
  aircraft.

REFERENCE SENT ON REQUEST

ROY CHURNUTT
40 Maple Road
Princeton, New Jersey 08540
(609) 921-2329

OBJECTIVE: To apply my expertise in computer programming, mathematical
             analysis, and problem solving to new and challenging projects.

SUMMARY: More than 20 years participation in government-funded research
             toward developing a new source of energy through controlled
             thermonuclear fusion. Expert in scientific computer programming
             and mathematical analysis. Designer of mathematical models
             for problem interpretation and solution. Author and contributor
             to published technical papers.

KNOWLEDGE OF AND EXPERIENCE IN:

        *FORTRAN, PL/1

        *Interactive computer systems: CDC Cyber 172 (NOS)
                                          vm370, DEC PDP 10
                                          NMFECC at Livermore, CA

        *Batch systems on IBM 360/91, CDC Cyber 172

        *Libraries and packages: IMSL, SSP, SORT, PERT

PROFESSIONAL EXPERIENCE:

1960 to   PLASMA PHYSICS LABORATORY, PRINCETON UNIVERSITY,
Present   Princeton, New Jersey

             Scientific Computer Programmer/Mathematical Analyst

        *   Member of support team for government-funded controlled
            thermonuclear fusion research

        *   Analyze raw output from a data acquisition system connected
            to a large fusion machine

        *   Write and run FORTRAN programs to solve differential equa-
            tions, make numerical approximations and produce graphic
            output

        *   Interpret problem, establish method of solution and
            translate data to computer language for intermediate and
            final analysis

            - Interact with physicists and engineers
            - Produce necessary documentation for programs
            - Meet deadlines for material to be included in papers
              published in technical journals and/or presented at
              conferences by senior researchers

ROY CHURNUTT/2

1957-60   UNIVERSITY OF WISCONSIN

               Graduate Teaching Assistant

               * Taught mathematics to undergraduate students

1956-57   RAND CORPORATION, Santa Monica, California

               Programmer/Analyst

               * Checked out and wrote programs in the Air Force's SAGE
                  computer system on the IBM ANFSQ/7

1952   U.S. NAVY (NEW YORK NAVAL SHIPYARD), Brooklyn, New York

               Physicist

               * Conducted photometric tests of lighting devices prior to
                  purchase by U.S. Navy

MILITARY: UNITED STATES ARMY, Guided Missile Equipment (Radar)
               12/53 - 9/55 (Honorably discharged)

EDUCATION: University of Wisconsin
               1957-60 Post-graduate work toward PhD in Mathematics

               University of Wisconsin
               1956 MS, Mathematics

               City College of New York
               1952 BS, Physics

LANGUAGES: Read some French, German, and Spanish

RECOGNITION IN PUBLICATIONS (Partial List):

1984   - T. L. Chu and Y.C. Lee: "Energy Confinement Comparison of
                 Ohmically Heated Stellarators to Tokamaks"

1982   - S. Suckewer and H. Fishman: "Conditions for Soft X-Ray Lasing
                 Action in a Confined Plasma Column"

1981   - J. Sredniawski, S.S. Medley and H. Fishman: "Vacuum System
                 Transient Simulator User's Manual for PPLCC Cyber System"

1977   - S. von Goeler et al: "Thermal X-Ray Spectra and Impurities
                 in the ST-Tokamak" (Nuclear Fusion)

References upon request

RÉSUMÉ OF

Roberta Yungki
4026 27th Avenue
Tucson, Arizona 85721
(602) 521-7707

EDUCATION

University of Arizona, Tucson, Arizona   1977 - 1978
Calculus, PL1 Courses; Grade Average B

Control Data Institute, Phoenix, Arizona   1/76 - 9/77
Certificate of Graduation in Programming. Languages: Assembler, Fortran,
RPG, Cobol; Grade Average A.

Arizona State University, Tempe, Arizona   9/70 - 12/74
Major - Kindergarten/Primary Education; Minor - Library Science
B.A.; Grade Average B

Company-Sponsored Course
DOS/VS Operating System and JCL; OS/VS1 Operating System and JCL; MVS
Operating System and JCL; Power JCL; CICS; DMS; ICCF; VOLLIE; VSAM; Easy-
trieve; Panvalet

EXPERIENCE

Dobbs Advertising, Inc., Tucson, Arizona   1982 - Present
Senior Programmer Analyst. Responsibilities include total responsibility
for the installation of McCormack & Dodge's Accounts Payable System.
Environment consists of an IBM 4341 operating DOS/VSE under Power, On-Line
Vollie and Librarian, using ADR DB/DC.

Goodyear Tire Co., Phoenix, Arizona   1981 - 1982
Programmer Analyst, Sales and Marketing. Implementation and design of
Inventory and Sales conversions for new division, using Cobol and RPG.
Analyzed, designed, coded, and tested new interim marketing system for
product usage. Environment consisted of IBM 370/158 operating DOS/VSE
under Power, On-Line Vollie and Librarian.

American Association of Insurance Systems, Phoenix, Arizona   1979 - 1981
Senior Associate Programmer Analyst. Analysis and re-design of Quarterly
Auto System. Maintained and enhanced Cobol, RPG, and Bal programs. Trained
team members in standards, methods, and new programming techniques. Environment: IBM 370/158 DOS/VSE under Power, On-Line ICCF.

Clover Manufacturing, Scottsdale, Arizona   1978 - 1979
Programmer, Marketing & Revenue Section. Maintained and enhanced Cobol
programs. Assisted in a study to sell Clover's property using Easytrieve.
Environment: IBM 370/158 OS/VS1, Panvalet.

Gotham Knitting Mills, Tucson, Arizona   9/77 - 11/78
Programmer/Programmer Trainee. Responsible for Payroll and Accounts Payable
Systems. Was back-up for Fixed Asset software package. Environment:
IBM 370/135 DOS under GRASP.

REFERENCES UPON REQUEST

MARGARET YORK

620 North Illinois Street   Arlington, Virginia 22205   (202) 847-6721
(703) 874-1000

SUMMARY: Applications specialist with the following experience:

- Skilled in PL/1, FORTRAN, BASIC, JCL, OS Utilities, MODEL 204 DBMS, XEROX 9700 Printing System, Assembler concepts, COBOL reading, structured methods, top-down design and development, speaking, writing, teaching.

- Supervised 1-3 programmers.

- Designed and programmed DBMS application of 300 modules.

- Made customer site studies and wrote study reports.

- Developed high-throughput utility for authors to type own texts and receive computer-printed formatted manuscripts.

- Worked in application areas: Federal Budget, Scientific Programming, Administrative Systems.

EDUCATION: BA Long Island University, New York 1967
Mathematics major

EXPERIENCE: PROGRAMMER/ANALYST. Dept. of the Interior, Washington, D.C.

1976 -   Designed and programmed Database Systems relating the
present   federal budget, laws, Congressional committees; user-
friendly, table-driven. Supervised junior programmers
for several years. Analyzed legislative information
process; wrote study reports of legislative clerk
offices. Devised and programmed utility for authors
to type papers into TSO/SPF and receive formatted manuscripts printed on the XEROX 9700.

6/67-9/76   ASSOCIATE PROGRAMMER. UNIVAC, Allentown, Pennsylvania
Wrote compiler modules. Wrote and converted aerospace
programs. Wrote and installed time accounting programs.
Used automated module library system. Wrote programming
production library plan. Wrote MIS user manuals. Worked
on suggestion processing system.

REFERENCES: On Request

Willing to relocate

June Brown
30 Broad Street
Atlanta, Georgia 30397
home: (404) 821-5994
work: (404) 532-4148

PROFESSIONAL OBJECTIVE: A challenging position as analyst/programmer
in design/development of commercial/business
applications.

EDUCATION:

1971   University of Chicago, Chicago, Illinois
BA: Major, Psychology - Minor, Chemistry

1980   Certificate in Computer Science (2-year program
coupled with previous degree equivalent to Bachelor's
in C.S.) Curriculum included: Data Structures,
Structure & Programming of Software Systems,
Operating Systems, Structure & Definition of
Higher Level Languages, Computer Architecture,
Math, Artificial Intelligence, COBOL, PASCAL,
ASSEMBLER.

HARDWARE/SOFTWARE: IBM 3033, 370/158, OS/MVS, OS/VS-1, CDC Cyber
172, NOS, TSO/SPF, PANVALET On-line, ADS (on-line
design guide) EASYTRIEVE, IMS DB/DC, COBOL,
BAL

PROFESSIONAL EXPERIENCE:

6-81-Present   STATE FARM INSURANCE CO., Atlanta, Georgia
30327
Lead Programmer/Analyst - Analyze, design, program
and implement on-line IMS programs to access
and update an IMS data base for agent (personnel
history, sales records, etc.) and agency records
(sales records, demographics, costs, etc.).
This large batch system uses IMS bridges for
updating and retrieval. Assist co-worker with
programming and debugging problems, teach classes
in software usage (EASYTRIEVE & Extended Checkpoint
Restart). Environment: IBM 3033, OS/MVS, TSO/SPF,
IMS DB/DC, ADS, EASYTRIEVE, COBOL.

6/78-6/81   STATE OF MAINE, Augusta, Maine 04330
Programmer (University of Maine, 6/80-6/81)
- Analysis, design, programming and implementation
of Batch and BMP IMS/COBOL programs to access
and update an IMS data base for student records.

PROFESSIONAL EXPERIENCE
(continued)

Environment: IBM 370/158, OS/MVS, TSO/SPF, IMS DB/DC, COBOL, BAL

<u>Programmer</u> (Dept. of Economic Security, 6/79-6/80)
- Analysis and programming of programs to access and update the liability determination and experience rating subsystems of the unemployment tax system. Also heavily involved in debugging and fixing converted ISAM to VSAM process programs. Environment: IBM 370/158, OS/VS-1, PANVALET, COBOL, BAL.

<u>Programmer</u> (University of Maine, 6/78-6/79)
- Study and test of new versions of data base software and compilers; consultant to students and faculty with programming, writing of utility software for general use. Environment: CDC Cyber 172, NOS, DBMS, System 2000, SIR, DMS 170, COBOL, COMPASS Assembler.

HOBBIES:

Painting, Swimming, Jogging

Willing to Relocate

References on Request

Helen Hanson
29 Cove Neck Road
Hartford, Connecticut 06131
  (203) 921-6626

OBJECTIVE: A position in a development environment with interests in
                  but not limited to:

                      * Software Analysis
                      * Evaluation
                      * Design
                      * Programming
                      * Supervision

EDUCATION: University of Vermont
                  M.A. Philosophy   1978

                  Dartmouth College
                  B.A. Philosophy   1976
                  Magna Cum Laude

HARDWARE: IBM 3080 series; MC68000; WICAT Microprocessors

SOFTWARE: OS/MVS2; CICS; JCL; TSO/SPF; VSAM; PANVALET; IDCAMS;
                  NATURAL; UNIX; INTERTEST; EDF; SDSF

LANGUAGES: COBOL; C

EXPERIENCE: THE HARTFORD INSURANCE CO., Hartford, Connecticut
                  Senior Programmer Analyst (November 1983 to Present)

5/78 -   * Evaluate Natural Language for insurance rating
Present   environment.
                  * Designed and implemented reinsurance reporting system.
                  * Redesign insurance rating and policy processing system.

                  Programmer Analyst (November 1982 to November 1983)

                  * Developed and instituted a COBOL/JCL course for
                     insurance analysts.
                  * Conducted feasibility study for implementing an
                     interactive, vendor-written package.
                  * Designed and implemented an automated library system
                     for a MC68000-based system.
                  * Developed and presented a plan for a rate quote system.
                  * Evaluated a software and data management package for
                     a rate quote system.

continued.....

Senior Programmer (November 1981 to November 1982)

* Programmed, tested, and documented an interactive premium system.
* Developed program specifications and control procedures for a CICS-based system.
* Coordinated activities between user departments and field for software implementation.
* Responsible for DASD management in an interactive environment.

Programmer (November 1980 to November 1981)

* Coded JCL and COBOL modules for a batch reporting system.
* Responsible for production support.
* Coordinated a complete forms revision with the user area and code modifications to programs and JCL.

Junior Programmer (May 1978 to November 1980)

* Updated existing programs with user-specified revisions.
* Coordinated a complete forms revision with the user area and code modifications to programs and JCL.

References upon request.

JACK L. GRIMES
670 MANNAKEE STREET   ROCKVILLE, MD 20850
Home: [301] 340-4801   Office: [202] 389-1602

STRENGTHS: Data Base Management Systems. . .Technical and Marketing Support. . .Systems Analysis. . .Client/User Interface. . .Technical Editing and Writing. . .Training. . .Report Design and Generation

EDUCATION: B.A., Marketing and Computer Science, University of Maryland, 1982

Basic System 2000, CDC INSTITUTE, 1979

HARDWARE: IBM 3033,370; VAX 11/780; UNIVAC 1108

SOFTWARE: COBOL, SYSTEM 2000, JCL, UTILITIES, TSO, MVS, OS/VS, PLEX, VMS, SEED, EXEC 8

NOTE: Current Secret Clearance.

EXPERIENCE:
1980 - Present   SYSTEMS CONSULTANTS, INC., Rockville, MD

Senior Analyst: For the U.S. Army RASDA Project, as part of IBM's S/370-MVS, System 2000 Data Base Management System. Create reports using the System 2000 DBMS report writer feature. Involved in string generator and string conversion from IBM V.2.80 to V.2.90. Applications have included IBM/SMF accounting data, airplane parts tracking, procurement and contracts accounting data. Data bases used were AMEN, DB, DMDCS, ICRL, PMP, PROCURE, REPAIRABLES.

Participated in the design and programming of the Depot Originated Jobs (DOJ) System. Wrote the DOJ Edit Program and the accompanying specifications using COBOL. Also wrote COBOL programs for other RASDA systems.

As part of the RASDA project, produced documentation for the RASDA Initial Operating Capability (I.O.C.). Wrote a voluminous amount of queries and the documentation used to test the Data Base Administration (DBA) Subsystem. Was also involved in producing the Operations and Maintenance Manual documents for several other RASDA modules.

As a member of a programming team converted CDC COBOL 1968 programs to 1974 IBM COBOL.

Wrote a PLEX program for the Department of the Interior project that produced several Comparative Financial Analysis Reports using the System 2000 Contracts Data Base.

Worked on an Analytical Maintenance Program using a parts tracking SEED Data Base running on a DEC VAX 11/780 under control of VMS operating system.

Implemented a Personnel System Data Base for DOT using IDMS DC on VAX 11/780 and IBM.

1978-1980   LONGFELLOW RESEARCH, INC. Baltimore, MD

Senior Data Base Analyst: For the U.S. Department of Health, Education and Welfare, Office of Policy Development and Research (PD&R) as part of the UNIVAC 1108, CDC, SYSTEM 2000 Data Base Management System. Involved in data archiving, data base backup and recovery, security, password generation, data base definition, data base design, and prototyping. Responsible for customer contact with HEW/PD&R office directors, division directors and government technical representatives. As link between data base and HEW personnel, determined HEW requirements; ascertained HEW needs for future or special purpose reports; designed and created reports; and trained client in system capabilities. Periodically analyzed data base and identified new elements, productions runs, and alternate SYSTEM 2000 tests to improve reports and data retrieval. Provided SYSTEM 2000 training and guidance to junior data base analysts with regard to data base maintenance and customer interface.

1974-1978   N.C.R. INC. Baltimore, MD

Proposal Coordinator: (1978) For the Marketing Services Unit, had full responsibility for editing and coordinating proposals, capabilities packages, company resumes, and project documentation. Assumed full responsibility for monitoring text and graphics through production cycle to final printing. Had the additional responsibility of proofreading and quality checking work produced by the corporation, graphics, and printing departments. Interfaced with technical staff and major publications users to assist scheduling of work through facility.

REFERENCES: On Request

Stanley Y. Bennett
12 Central Street, South
Omaha, Nebraska   68114

(402) 456-0976 (Home)
(402) 451-4555 (Work)

STRENGTHS: Systems Analysis, Design and Implementation...Requirements
Analysis...Personnel/Payroll Systems...User/Client
Interface

EDUCATION: M.B.A., Information Systems Technology (emphasis on
Finance and Information Systems); GEORGETOWN
UNIVERSITY, 1981.

B.S., Mathematics; NORTHWESTERN UNIVERSITY, 1975.

HARDWARE: IBM 3033, 370/158/155; Univac 1100/80; CDC 6400; 3M
Linolex word processor

SOFTWARE: COBOL, FORTRAN, BASIC, TSO/SPF, PANVALET, Method/1, DMS
1100, Image, H-P DBMS. Academic knowledge of telecommunications, ADABAS, TOTAL, Model 204, IMS.

EXPERIENCE:

3/81-Present   CENTRAL ELECTRONICS, INC., Omaha, Nebraska

Systems Analyst: Responsible for major enhancements and
maintenance of personnel, benefit, and profit-sharing
application systems in an IBM 370/158 and 3033 environment utilizing COBOL, TSO/SPF, PANVALET and Method/1.

10/77-3/81   B.R.S. INFORMATION CORP., Falls Church, Virginia

Systems Analyst: Designed personnel/payroll system for
BRS headquarters and divisional personnel using data
base technology.

Performed requirements analysis for system to charge
back telephone costs to departments using the DIMENSION
PBX telephone system.

Designed and wrote specifications for library routing
and acquisition system for implementation on a Univac
1100/80. Responsibilities included performance of a requirements survey and presentation of system proposal to
user management for project approval.

7/76-10/77   BRADLEY TRUST COMPANY, Waltham, Massachusetts

Systems Analyst: Developed computer systems for procurement, administrative, and economic divisions.
Designed and implemented interactive financial applications on Honeywell hardware.

Supervised intern in all phases of system development
functions during development and design of nationwide
retrieval and reporting system.

Developed and conducted workshops with up to 20 parti-
cipants on time-sharing computer for an on-line application.

Programmed system to determine benefits of competitive
procurement of telecommunications services. Responsible
for maintenance, user liaison of software.

Assisted operating management in the selection of word
processing equipment. Advised trainee in performing
word processing feasibility studies.

5/75-6/76   BEDFORD COMPUTER ASSOCIATES, Bedford, Massachusetts

Programmer: Wrote FORTRAN programs on CDC 6400 to provide senior scientists with solutions to acoustical
problems. Modified and documented existing software.
Provided graphical analysis of results. (Cooperative
assignment).

Summer 1974   AZTEC, INC., Chicago, Illinois

Programmer: Tested and implemented FORTRAN programs
on an IBM 370/155 for analysis of optics research
studies. Produced holograms on a Laser Scanner Recorder. Performed an analysis of department terminal
usage. Revised operations manual for Laser Scanner
Recorder. (Cooperative assignment).

References on request

Barbara Levinworth
69 Stonehedge Road
Wayland, Ma.
(617) 358-4169

U.S. CITIZEN

SUMMARY   Heavy involvement in the C language, UNIX area of
          programming both in Systems and Applications.

HARDWARE/ C-programming language, PASCAL, BASIC, PL/1, IBM assembler,
SOFTWARE   COBOL, 6502 assembly language, and 8080 assembly. Operating
           systems: UNIX, TSS, APPLE II DOS. DEC VAX 11/780, IBM,
           WE 3B 2)S, APPLE II.

EXPERIENCE MCI Communications, Inc., Burlington, Ma.

1979 to   Software Engineer
Present   Presently involved in designing, implementing, and debugging
           a project to interconnect a fault and load tester through
           a DEC VAX computer to the five ESS (Electronic Switching
           Systems). The tester inserts faults, loads the switch,
           and accumulates the data into a spooler for later analysis.

           Wrote a complete data-base management network service
           on a project charged with the job of designing and imple-
           menting a data-base system aimed at the four ESS (Electronic
           Switching System) developers and support group. Wrote new
           programs, debugged and enhanced existing programs used for
           locating and updating translations to the 4 ESS.

           Participated in the design of a model to evaluate Human
           Factors input toward teleconferences. Functioned as
           applications programmer to write a full DBMS including shared
           files, transaction processing, logging, etc.

           Pennsylvania Bell, Inc., Philadelphia, Pa.

1967 to   Transmission Craftperson
1979   Maintained the transmission quality of the long haul cable
           systems used. Worked as a central office technician on
           high frequency multiplex systems (Analog & Digital). Worked
           as a licensed radio operator on such systems as Collins,
           WE TD-2, WE TD-3, and Linkurt to ensure quality from point
           to point transmission.

EDUCATION Temple University, Philadelphia, Pa.
           B.S. Computer Science 1979-1983

DONALD CHU . 100 Hidden Lake Drive Apt. 18L . North Brunswick, NJ 08902
Home: (201) 297-4340   Business: (215) 293-5261

OBJECTIVE

Position involving design, implementation, and management of information systems; special interest in the management of a R&D environment.

EDUCATION

George Washington University: B.S. in Business Administration; graduated Summa Cum Laude and ranked 1st in School of Business Administration class of 200+ and 2nd in University graduating class of 1200+; Major: Economics, Minor: Computer Science.

HONORS

- Rhodes Scholarship nominee
- President, Financial Managers Association Honor Society, 1981
- Wall Street Journal Award for excellence in the field of Finance and Securities Analysis recipient
- International Youth in Achievement Award for Scholastic Excellence recipient

PROFESSIONAL EXPERIENCE

4/82 - Present   Prescut Videotronics, New York, NY

Software Engineer. Responsible for design and implementation of prototype software/hardware interface system, involving APPLE II microcomputer system and animated filming stand in a R&D environment; also responsible for operation of animation stand during filming projects; daily exposure to video (interactive videodisc, videotape), film, and animated graphics technologies; I/O devices; hardware interfacing techniques/protocols (esp. asynchronous communication); and 6502 Assembly language. Expertise in PASCAL.

9/80 - 4/82   Data Services Corporation, St. Louis, MO

Programmer/Analyst II. Analysis, design, and implementation of transactional-batch and on-line DBMS query systems; expertise in PLI, COBOL, ADABAS (database), COMPLETE (TP monitor), NATURAL (interactive programming language), ISAM file organization, list processing, IBM OS/VS1 JCL, CMS, EDGAR, IBM's Ex-Editor; knowledge of Fortran, IBM Assembly and Macro languages, and SPSS.

6/78 - 8/80
(Part-time)

Financial Research Assistant. Statistical analysis for research project in financial portfolio theory.

References upon request.

JOHN TUMINO, 25 NORTHRIDGE ROAD, OLD GREENWICH, CONNECTICUT 06870
Home: (203) 637-6653   Office: (212) 980-8573

EDUCATION: University of Colorado, Boulder
                      M.S. Computer Science; 1977

                      Emerson College, Boston, Massachusetts
                      B.A. Computer Science (magna cum laude, Phi Beta Kappa);
                      1976

COMPUTER   Ada, C, PASCAL, Fortran, BASIC, LISP, IBM Assembler,
LANGUAGES: MACRO-10

COMPUTERS: PDP 11/70, IBM 370, CDC 7600

EMPLOYMENT   MODERN SYSTEMS, INC., New Haven Connecticut 06504
HISTORY:

9/78-Present   Software Engineer
                      Support Software Led the design of a linker and library
                      system for the Ada Integrated Environment. Managed a
                      group of four people. Specified, designed, and imple-
                      mented a debugger for a high-level language. Managed
                      a group of four people in the design and implementation
                      phases.
                      Language Design Designed a Command Language for a
                      Minimal Ada Programming Support Environment (MAPSE).
                      This MAPSE Command Language (MCL) combined Ada-like
                      features, such as flow control commands, with UNIX-like
                      command-level functionality, such as I/O redirection
                      and execution of commands in the background or as
                      co-routines.
                      Support Software Designed and implemented a debugger
                      for an Ada compiler. This debugger, itself written in
                      Ada, provides the user with the ability to set break-
                      points at arbitrary Ada statements, view and modify
                      variables, and modify the flow of control of the program
                      being debugged.
                      Compilers & Support Software Designed and implemented
                      a facility for separate compilation of PASCAL code
                      modules. This facility builds a database of global
                      named objects which can then be imported into code
                      modules, as well as tracking which code modules must
                      be recompiled if a global variable is changed. Also
                      implemented built-in functions in the semantics of
                      the associated PASCAL code compiler.
                      Operating Systems Member of the executive group which
                      oversees the operation of a PDP-11 running UNIX. Respon-
                      sible for improvements to the system such as installing
                      accounting, implementing Harvard Teco and adding a new
                      system call to determine if any data is ready to be input
                      from a user teletype.

EMPLOYMENT
HISTORY
(Continued)

<u>Operating Systems & Networking</u> Systems Programmer for
the UNIX operating system. Made various efficiency
improvements in the Network Control Program which
interfaces to the ARPA network. Also designed and
implemented performance improvements in UNIX's
interprocess communications mechanism, which led to
a five-fold improvement in the throughput of UNIX
pipes and ports. Also performed extensive throughput
measurements on a secure subnet of the ARPA net.

5/77-9/78

UNIVERSITY OF CALIFORNIA, Berkeley, California 94721
<u>Research Assistant in Database Design</u> Developed a
software package for a PDP 11/70 for the management and
analysis of a database consisting of musical information.
The data was organized into a hierarchical database.
Record fields were either assigned a fixed space within
each record or were placed in an extension segment on
a per-occurrence basis, depending on the frequency
count for the particular field. Developed a query
language for the database to select records satisfying
an arbitrary Boolean expression. Was also responsible
for coordinating a staff of undergraduate programmers.

References on Request

HOWARD D. PAPPAS
10 Hall Avenue
Freehold, NJ 07728
(201) 780-1576
(201) 780-2251

SUMMARY
Experienced in design of data processing systems, word processing systems,
automation of programming and operation research analysis. Have had over
15 years programming experience using Z80 and 8080 assemblers, IBM assembler and SPL, FORTRAN, Honeywell Level-6 and SPD-20 assemblers, 8086
assembler, C language, UNIX/lib. Also worked with PDP assembler, CDC
assembler, BASIC. Developed methods of calculations in the fields of
queueing theory, coding for data transfer, combinatorial tasks and statistics.

EDUCATION
Massachusetts Institute of Technology, Cambridge, MA
Ph.D. in Computer Sciences - 1962

Lafayette University, Easton, PA
Master of Science in Electrical Engineering - 1953
Bachelor of Science in Electrical Engineering - 1951

EMPLOYMENT HISTORY
May 1982 to Present
R.C.A. LABORATORIES/Trenton, NJ

POSITION: Staff Principal Software Engineer
DUTIES: Developed high-performance SORT systems on base of Z80
              Assembler for word processing, database, and BASIC
              language systems. Developed methods and programs of
              interactive tabular calculations (extended spreadsheet
              system).

February 1981 to May 1982
XEROX/ Elmira, NY

POSITION: Principal Software Engineer
DUTIES: Developed simulation models for performance analysis of
              computerized local networks: the simulator of on-line
              multi-users system for word processing and office auto-
              mation systems on SPD-20 microcomputer and Level-6; the
              simulator of on-line multi-user system for automatic
              teller machine system; the emulator for performance
              analysis of on-line system; the converter for automatic
              generation of tests; theoretical calculations of
              queueing processes in on-line systems.

June 1980 to February 1981
TELEX INTERNATIONAL/Binghamton, NY

POSITION: Senior Computer Programming Analyst
DUTIES: Developed application systems and a number of separate
            programs on DEC-10: the report generation system includ-
            ing special language for description and connection of
            text and numerical data; the input system for loading
            of information and description of database (specifically
            for 1022 system); the special system for connection
            between report generation and typesetting systems.

1967 to 1979
B & G RESEARCH CENTER/Binghamton, NY

POSITION: Head of Department of Information & Computation Systems
DUTIES: Developed a language for automation of programming for
            routine data processing (tabular economic and experi-
            mental information). Designed systems software using
            IBM Assembler: database management for interconnected
            tabular data in scientific and business applications
            (calculations, statistics, report generation); multi-
            dimensional analysis system for qualitative data;
            retrieval & editing system for data classification.
            Developed methods and programs for priority control
            and linear optimization of queueing processes and for
            automatic classification of scientific and statistical
            information.

1962 to 1967
INSTITUTE OF ELECTRONIC & ELECTRICAL ENGINEERS/New York, NY

POSITION: Systems Analyst/Systems Programmer
DUTIES: Developed teleinformation systems and calculation methods
            for queueing processes on the systems of invariable
            holding time and methods for redundant coding applied to
            data transfer and computing.

PATENTS
Hold two patents.

REFERENCES
Furnished upon request.

John Hawkins, C.P.A.   250 Main Street, Apartment 3-G Millburn, New Jersey 07041
Home (201) 379-4761   Office (212) 790-5206

CAREER
OBJECTIVE: DESIGN AUTOMATION PROGRAMMER/SOFTWARE ENGINEERING

EDUCATION: Williams College, Williamsport, Massachusetts
                    Bachelor of Science, Mathematics, 1980

                    WORKSHOPS:
                    Gate Array Seminar, Stanford University, 1983
                    Effective Writing Workshop, Data General, 1983
                    Information Modeling, Yourdon, Inc., 1983
                    User Computer Interfaces, Data General, 1982
                    Basic Electronics, Computechnics, Inc., 1981
                    Fundamentals of Microprocessors and Microcomputers,
                    Data General, 1981

TECHNICAL
STRENGTHS: SOFTWARE: FORTRAN, PL/1, PASCAL, Assembly for Motorola
                    6800 and 8080/8085, APL, COBOL.

                    HARDWARE: 16 & 32 BIT Data General Eclipse Systems.

EXPERIENCE:

8/80 to   RCA AUTOMATED SYSTEMS, NEWARK, NJ
PRESENT   Design Automation, Software Engineer

                    Department supplies CAD tools for in-house LSI/PCB
                    design engineers.

                    Designed and implemented network consistency verifi-
                    cation program. Used in both LSI/PCB design cycles
                    for post-routing verification. Detects and reports
                    shorts and discontinuities.

                    Designed and implemented program used in calculating
                    media delays on LSI gate arrays. Provided listing of
                    metal lengths, capacitances, number of feedthru's for
                    each network. Also provided design totals, "N" worst
                    networks in each category, and cumulative/distributive
                    histograms. Used DG charting package Trendview.

                    Supported enhancement of LSI gate array physical de-
                    sign system. Primarily debugged library and routing
                    programs. Wrote functional and design specification
                    for graphical layout editor. Editor allows manual
                    placement and routing on PCB/LSI gate arrays. Tar-
                    geted to be commercially competitive. Design spec.

outlines the data structure, the use of binary search trees, and hashing functions.

Re-designed and provided support for design data base (DDB) maintenance program: Modified (add, delete, change) all aspects of the DDB. Algorithm modifying interconnections is a post-order tree traversal.

Built database schemas for DBMS, outlining entities, attributes, and related primary keys for physical design. Included process model of LSI physical design cycle.

Pioneered department's use of Yourdon structured analysis and design methodologies. Primary reference was "structured systems and specifications".

Performed product demonstrations of the PCB and LSI gate array design systems. Demonstrated schematic capture, manual placement, and routing.

Established and coordinated PCB designer user meetings. Monthly meetings between designers and tool developers. Acted as moderator.

References sent on request.

James Rivera
1046 Escondido Dr.
Dallas, Tx. 75231

OBJECTIVE: A position in a technologically advanced UNIX based environment which allows the opportunity to utilize a background in operating systems, software tools, and microcode development.

EDUCATION: M.S. ELECTRICAL and COMPUTER ENGINEERING 1982
California Institute of Technology

B.S. ELECTRICAL and COMPUTER ENGINEERING 1980
California Institute of Technology

SUMMARY OF TECHNICAL EXPERIENCE
Strong understanding of the internals of the UNIX operating system, as well as a strong familiarity with use of the various tools available on UNIX operating systems.

SOFTWARE: 'C' PASCAL FORTRAN BASIC ASSEMBLER (Z/80, 8080) RATFOR LEX YACC
operating systems: UNIX RSX/11M CP/M OS/MVS

HARDWARE: DEC PDP 60,44,34,11/23 8080 Z/80 AMDAHL
Familiar with the machine architecture view of PDP-11 systems, such as the operation of the memory management subsystems, kernel level privileges, the interrupt processing subsystem, and the way in which the architecture affects the design of system level software and portability.

EXPERIENCE: SONY SYSTEMS, INC., Dallas, Tx.

Software Engineer

  *Wrote and modified device drivers for several types of devices on the UNIX operating system, including tape, disk, and serial devices.
  *Administrator for a BETA test site of the Berkeley 2.8 BSD version of UNIX, which required debugging the kernel, several system level programs, and various tools.
  *Utilized the LEX and YACC languages to implement parsers for 3 separate projects, including a compiler, a special purpose assembler, and an IC layout specification system.

September
1982 to
present

Current work involves microcode assembler and logic simulator design for a special PLA driven microsequence architecture. Designed and implemented a software system to drive graphics display devices,

plotters, and a pattern generator from CIF
input for integrated circuit design.

Also familiar with structured programming methods
as well as an engineering perspective on the
software design process. This includes state
machine representation of software, formal grammatical methods of describing input languages, and
the modular decomposition approach to projects.

Summer   LSI CORPORATION, Austin, Tx.
1982

Systems Administrator
As a member of the company's "port" team, acted as
a systems administrator, porting the "adb" debugger
and providing technical support with respect to the
UNIX system and its operation. Also taught end
users how to use and administer various company
systems.

References upon request.

GARY GRAY ˙ 86-11 94th Ave. ˙ Jackson Hts., NY 11372 ˙(212) 672-6606

POSITION: COMPUTER PROGRAMMER

HARDWARE: IBM 3033, IBM 360/22, IBM 370/168, AMDAHL 470/V6
1403 Printer, 2540R Reader, 2311 Disk Drive,
2415 Tape Drive, Digital Decwriter II, Datamedia
Elite CRT, PDP 11/40 minicomputer, Singer ten,
Prime minicomputer, Nixdorft minicomputer

SOFTWARE: COBOL, ASSEMBLER (BAL), ASSEMBLER (DMF-II); working
knowledge of PRG II, PL-1, BASIC, FORTRAN, IBM/OS,
Teleprocessing, Hardware Systems and Systems
Analysis

EXPERIENCE:

Current   BASIC RESEARCH AND DEVELOPMENT, Long Island, NY
Minicomputer Assembler Programming/Data Processing Coordinator
(Report directly to Senior V.P. in charge of Engineering)

* Designed and implemented customized data entry programs
for clients including a major New York utility

* Assist Chief Systems Analyst in design of upcoming
projects

  - Set up computerized library control system
    for use in and out of house

  - Worked on the development of software for users
    with turnkey expectations

  - Attended regular meetings with D.P. personnel at
    utilities companies to assess their software
    needs

1980   HARDACH TRAVEL SERVICE, New York, NY
Mini-Computer Operator (On-line system)

* Directed department responsible for computation and issuance
of invoices, credit and debit statements

* Issued international airline tickets on Nova system connected to Sabre system

* Developed accounting program in COBOL; saves company
500 work-hours annually

* Worked independently; set own schedule and work hours

1979   SMITH, BARNEY, HARRIS, UPHAM & COMPANY, New York, NY
Lead Operator - Data Entry

* Responsible for verification of work of 40-member
computer staff

* Within four months, achieved speed levels which
surpassed all others in department

1974-1979   1001 DISCOUNT STORES, DBA EA DISCOUNT, Richmond Hill, NY
             <u>Manager</u>

             *   Increased annual revenues from zero base of $500,000
                 per store in six year period

             *   Installed NCR electronic digital cash registers in
                 both branches

             (Worked while attending school)

EDUCATION: BARUCH COLLEGE, New York, NY
             1980 - Certificate: Computer Programming and Systems
                                   Design

             NEW YORK UNIVERSITY, New York, NY
             1/80-5/80 - COBOL

             QUEENSBOROUGH COMMUNITY COLLEGE, Queens, NY
             1975-76 - Course concentration: Business Administration

             YORK COLLEGE, CUNY, New York, NY
             1973-75 - Course concentration: Music Composition

             Working knowledge of Spanish

PERSONAL: Willing to relocate; free to travel

Jay Oliver
685 Summer Street
Austin, Texas 78745

Home Phone: (512) 203-5681
Business Phone: (512) 986-2384

EDUCATION

1976   M.I.T., Cambridge, Massachusetts 02139
              M.S. Applied Math

1974   Rice University, Houston, Texas 77001
              BA Mathematics
              Magna Cum Laude

HARDWARE   IBM 370/155, UNIVAC
SOFTWARE   BAL, JCL, DYL-260, ISAM, COBOL, FORTRAN

EXPERIENCE
June 1980
to Present   Bankers Trust Co., Austin, Texas 78760

              PROGRAMMER/ANALYST

              Personally responsible for the design, programming,
              testing, and implementation of the following appli-
              cations: savings, demand deposits, certificates of
              deposit, installment loans. Programming is in BAL
              on an IBM 370/155.

              Duties include 30% new development and design and
              70% maintenance. Use DYL-260 for report develop-
              ment and file handling. Worked closely with JCL
              and ISAM files.

              Additionally responsible for adding new clients to
              the services, mergers, and conversions. Work with
              an analyst to update fields and delete redundant
              data.

May 1977   Data Language Corporation, Austin, Texas 78712
to June 1980
              SENIOR PROGRAMMER/TECHNICAL SUPPORT

              Responsible as the supervisor of 1-3 programmers and
              as an individual contributor in the enhancement,
              programming, testing, and implementation of the
              following applications:

                  -Accounts Payable
                  -Accounts Receivable
                  -Cash Posting
                  -Purchase Order
                  -Inventory Posting

              Programmed in an assembler language in the on-line
              programming department.

References on request

MANAGEMENT

Laura Jane Simmons
220 West Street
Hendersville, N.C. 27208

Home: (919) 421-1562
Work: (919) 472-2900

AREAS OF
APPLICATION

Information Retrieval Systems; Data Base Management Systems; computerized information systems (bibliographic/non-bibliographic) design, implementation, computer operations management; systems programming; production services, operation and management of special application in Litigation Management Systems.

EDUCATION

B.S., Business Administration, University of Maryland

Experience
1978-present

INFORMATION RETRIEVERS, Hendersville, N.C. 27205
Director, Operations Support

Responsible for administrative and technical support of all major litigation projects for the Division. Also responsible for day-to-day management of all project personnel, providing for complete contract coverage while generating career opportunity and growth within the litigation support division.

Responsible for ensuring that operational needs are satisfied during contract negotiations and also that contractual obligations can be met from an operations standpoint.

Responsible for all project start-up activities following successful negotiations. This includes initial customer contact, staffing, design studies, and getting project to operational status so it can be turned over to on-going project personnel.

1976-1978

AMERICAN COMPUTERS, INC., Baltimore, Md. 21210
Director, Information Network Services

Total responsibility for cost center operations. This encompassed total business and technical management of all projects in the application area. Included were projects dealing with on-line retrieval, custom software installations, and litigation management specifically with U. S. Government Agencies. Some of the customers supported are: Environmental Protection Agency, Agency for Internal Development, and Department of Transportation.

1973-1976

DOCUMENTATIONS, INC., Baltimore, Md. 21201
Computer Specialist

Principal area of responsibility included assisting in the design and specification of the File Maintenance Subsystem. After three months, was promoted to Supervisor of the File Maintenance Activities, from which the completion of the design of the subsystem, conversion of existing files to the format, and the implementation of the full system were accomplished. In this regard, conducted several seminars and lectures on the user impact of the new system.

Most of the applications were classified in nature, but participated in the design of a multiprogramming executive for the CDC 3600. Also designed a simultaneous peripheral Processing Package utilizing the CDC 160-A as a slave to a master CDC 3600. Developed a training class for the UNIVAC 1224-A, which was presented to approximately 60 people.

Computer Languages

PL/1, ALC, COBOL, MARK IV, DBMS

Machines

IBM 1401, 7090, 360, 370
CDC 160-A, 1604, 3600
UNIVAC 490, 1224-A, PRIME 850

References available upon request.

ROBERT STEVENS
1573 Palm Springs Blvd.
Miami, Florida 33182
(305) 890-2177

**RELEVANT
EXPERIENCE:** 8 years experience in computer sciences field. Experience includes increasingly responsible positions within the areas of applications programming, systems design and development, project and task management, and computer operations.

HARDWARE	DBMSs	LANGUAGES	SYSTEMS & SOFTWARE
IBM 3033	SYSTEM 2000	COBOL	OS MVS & MVT
IBM 370/168	RAMIS	PL-1	SYSTEM 2000 PL-1
IBM 370/158	ADABAS	BASIC	LIBRARIAN
IBM 360/145	TOTAL		TSO/CLISTS
IBM 360/30			SPF
UNIVAC 1108			SUPERWYLBUR/MACRO
			PANVALET
			DOS
			JES 2
			HASP

**SECURITY
CLEARANCE:** *SECRET, previous clearance Interium Top Secret.

APPLICATIONS: Management Information Systems
Personnel Systems
Data Base Management Systems
Energy Resource Systems

**EXPERIENCE:
1978 to
Present**

INTERNATIONAL COMPUTER CORPORATION, Ft. Lauderdale, Florida
*Project Manager & Senior Programmer/Analyst - (1981 - Present)

Currently managing a staff of 25 programmers, analysts, statisticians, data technicians, and a journalist supporting the Florida Department of Energy/Energy Information Administration in the development and maintenance of survey processing systems. Experience includes project resource scheduling and planning, client liaison, quality control, recruiting and staffing, budget monitoring and tracking, and management of several subcontractors.

*Project Manager & Senior Programmer/Analyst - (1980 - 1981)
Responsible for recruiting and staffing, monitoring of individual task assignments, client liaison, status reporting, and supervisory duties of a project staff of 11 systems programmers and programmer/analysts. In addition, performed analysis, design, and development of a Personnel System in COBOL for the IBM 360/365 utilizing OS JCL, TSO, LIBRARIAN and RAMIS.

*Senior Programmer/Analyst - (1979 - 1980)
Assisted on a large systems development effort at the Rider Trucking Company. Responsible for analysis, design, programming, and validating of cover memo and information sheet software for beneficiary notices produced by the Automated Job Stream Version III. In addition, responsible for subsystem flowcharting and coding, systems testing, and extensive documentation. Programming was done in COBOL in an IBM 370/168, OS/MVS environment utilizing TSO with SPF and PANVALET.

        *Programmer/Analyst - (1978 - 1979)

For a multi-task effort at the Arco Oil Company for the design, development, implementation, and documentation of System 2000 and TOTAL data bases, and associated COBOL and SYSTEM 200 PL-1 programs in an IBM 370 environment utilizing OS/MVS JCL, TSO and SUPERWYLBUR. Experience includes writing COBOL programs, creating SYSTEM 2000 data bases and corresponding systems (using PL-1) for the Respondent Information System and a Gas Price Tracking system, and creating SUPERWYLBUR macros for the systems.

1972 to 1978	U. S. ARMY, Arizona *Programmer

Assisted in a system review of an existing batch management information system for tracking military personnel world wide. Prepared program coding changes, flow charts, documentation, and testing utilizing COBOL, EXEC 8 and SYSTEM 2000 in a UNIVAC 1108 environment.

ADP TRAINING CENTER: Various courses in UNIVAC and IBM Operating Principles: EXEC 8, OS and DOS JCL; SYSTEM 2000; RAMIS: TSO: Structured COBOL; and Systems Analysis.

References on request.

MATTHEW SILVERMAN ● 45-59 65th St. ● Woodside, NY 11377 ● (212) 786-3576

OBJECTIVE: Seek a challenging, shirtsleeves management position.

EDUCATION: <u>M.A.</u>, Mathematics, 1979
CUNY, New York City

<u>B.A.</u>, Mathematics, Magna Cum Laude, 1971
Hofstra University

HARDWARE: DEC 10, PDP 11/70; Honeywell 437; North Star Advantage

OPERATING
SYSTEMS: TOPS 10, RSTS/E, CP/M

SOFTWARE: FORTRAN, MACRO 10, BASIC, DBMS 10, COBOL, Pascal, CALL

HIGH LEVEL
SOFTWARE: Time Series Analysis, Financial Analysis, Graphics, Report Writer

EXPERIENCE:
1978-Present

CALL DATA CORPORATION, New York, NY

<u>Technical Manager</u> (1/83-Present)

* Manage a group of 18 software development and support professionals.

* Overall support and development responsibilities for a 15-million dollar multi-year Dedicated Service Contract with a major Bell Operating Company: 3 DEC-10 KL systems.

<u>Project Leader</u>, Communications Systems Division (1980-1982)

* Developed DIAL, an interactive, interpreted language used to model Telephone Networks.

* Overall support and development responsibilities for applications comprising 48% of District's revenues.

* Designed, developed, sold, and supported a Work Order Management System which partly replaced a Western Electric system which performs similar functions. Presidential-level attention in the client company resulted in the sale of a 3rd DEC-10 KL system.

* Managed the documentation of client's largest applications. Managed a group of 9 professionals.

<u>Applications Consultant</u>, Securities Division (1978-1980)

* Provided technical support and development services to all client locations in New York State outside of New York City.

Page 1 of 2

APPLICANT
Matthew Silverman
-2-

NON D.P. EXPERIENCE: 1971-1978	BROADHURST PUBLIC SCHOOLS
	Mathematics Instructor
ARTICLES:	"A C Program That Does Your Income Tax," <u>Creative Computing</u>, July 1978
	"A Documentation Standard for Local Applications," (Internal), June 1981
LANGUAGES WRITTEN:	DIAL, an interactive, interpreted language used to model Telephone Networks.
PROFESSIONAL:	Member ACM

PAUL RAYSON
(Confidential)
519 S. 4th Street
Edinburg, Texas 78539
Phone: Home: (512) 383-6655
Office: (512) 381-2515

EDUCATION	UNIVERSITY OF TEXAS: Phd. 1967 (Chemistry)
	NORTHWESTERN UNIVERSITY: MA. 1965 (Chemistry)
	TEMPLE COLLEGE: BA. 1965 (Chemistry)

OBJECTIVE

Management position in the system software area in a technically advanced environment.

**COMPUTER
EXPERIENCE
AND
INTERESTS**

IBM System/370 (VM/CMS, OS), PDP-11 (UNIX), DECsystem-20 (TOPS-20)
IBM Personal Computer (MS-DOS, Xenix), Zenith Z89 (CP/M)
Pascal, PL/I, AED, Ratfor, C, APL; S/370, DEC-20, 8080, 8086 assemblers

Management of the system development process
Language design, interpreters, preprocessors, non-procedural languages
Operating systems, process-to-process communication, networks
User-friendly interfaces to complex systems
Development of novel algorithms and systems for mathematical programming

**EMPLOYMENT
HISTORY
March 1980–
present:**

ACME DATA CORPORATION, Dallas, Texas

Manager of Systems Software
Responsible for the development and maintenance of basic software for building decision support systems, including DDS (a very comprehensive system for statistics and econometrics), and support of the Applications and Product programming groups. Recent achievements include:

* Release of an easy-to-use multi-dimensional report writing system

* Release of a multi-dimensional data access method in DDS

* Completion of software to allow a microcomputer-resident menu system to drive programs on a mainframe computer

* Release of a preprocessor for DDS's macro language

* Implementation of a mainframe-resident full screen editor

Was responsible for producing a version of DDS to run under VM/SP, and for many new product offerings and enhancements to DDS. Built up the Systems Software Group from two people to eight, and turned it into a truly productive entity by emphasizing good software development techniques and effective project management.

CREDITS & SURVEYS, New York City, New York

**May 1979-
March 1980:**

Director of Information Systems
Management and budgetary responsibility for development and operation of all corporate information systems. Directed the design and installation of a comprehensive on-line MIS to serve project managers and staff departments in the Chicago and New York offices.

Oct. 1977-
May 1979:

Director of Data Processing
Operational and budgetary responsibility for all survey data processing, in a department of 50 people with an annual budget of over $500,000. Specific achievements included implementation of a survey management information system, introduction of improved methods and procedures, contributions to winning proposals, and rejuvenation of a formerly moribund department.

Jan. 1974-
Sept. 1977:

INSTITUTE OF COMPUTER RESEARCH, Cleveland, Ohio.

Research Associate
Initially worked on implementation of a large-scale interactive linear programming system, with responsibility for major portions of the code. Subsequently led a group that designed a highly innovative and adaptable interactive linear programming system that featured a non-procedural model specification language. Also heavily involved with the computer realization of complex mathematical models, particularly in the energy field.

June 1970-
Dec. '74:

SHARPE RESEARCH ASSOCIATES, Cleveland, Ohio

Senior Programmer, Operations Research Department
Contributed to the design and coding of the integer programming portion of the PM operating system. Designed and implemented a new inversion algorithm for the system for 8100 series computers. Modified in-core FORTRAN compiler for efficient operation under the primary virtual storage operating system.

SCHOLARSHIPS
AND HONORS

Elected to Sigma Xi, University of Texas, Austin

President's Award, 1981, Acme Data Corporation

PROFESSIONAL
SOCIETIES

Association for Computing Machinery
IEEE Computer Society

References:

On Request

WILLIAM FREDERICKS, 314 SAN FERNANDO AVENUE, HOHOKUS, NEW JERSEY 07423
Telephone: (201)456-4921

SUMMARY
- Strong first- and second-level manager
- Extensive requirements analysis experience in diverse user environments
- Responsibility for long-range planning including cost/benefit and capacity analysis
- Hardware/software evaluation and selection
- In-depth systems software and applications background
- Highly motivated self-starter with strong interpersonal skills

EXPERIENCE

1971 to Present
ST. JOHN'S HOSPITAL, Montclair, N.J. 07042

(1980 to Present)
Assistant Director, MIS Planning and System Support
Supervisory responsibility for 2 managers and 30 professionals with functional responsibility for the daily operations of the data processing department including operations and systems.

Our computer services environment presently contains an IBM 370/148 and an IBM 4341 MOD II operating under DOS/VSE. Additional software consists of Taskmaster (teleprocessing monitor), IDMS (database management system), IDD (data dictionary), OLQ (on-line query), and IDMS/DC (teleprocessing monitor). Specific responsibilities include:

- purchasing and planning decisions affecting all software and hardware
- budget preparation and forecasting
- third party negotiations
- operation and system software staff
- user interface
- strategic and tactical planning
- training and education for all MIS personnel
- review database design

(1979 to 1980)
Acting Director, MIS
Supervisory responsibility for 36 data processing professionals with total responsibility for data processing including hardware, software, new systems, operations, systems design, and programming. Specifically responsible for the consolidation of the data processing department from 2 separate divisions into one comprehensive department.

Highlight: reorganized data processing through a reclassification and restructuring of the department, resulting in an increase in morale and productivity.

(1977 to 1979)   **Systems Software Manager**

Responsible for the supervision of 4 individuals and training of systems programmers and systems specialists including selecting outside education vendors and conducting in-house training programs. Also responsible for:

- recommending and purchasing software and hardware
- negotiations of third party contracts
- assisting users in selection of application software packages.

Highlight: increased computer capacity 100% with no increase in the hardware budget.

(1975 to 1977)   **Software Systems Specialist**

In this newly created position, responsible for the design, programming, and installation of new on-line systems, with database management system.

(1971 to 1975)   **Programmer/Analyst**

Joined St. John's Hospital as a computer operator, promoted to stated position responsible for the design and coding of several applications.

1964 to 1971   Served in the U.S. Army and held various non-data processing positions.

EDUCATION   Information Systems
Rutgers University

REFERENCE   On request

Robert Anderson
303 Front Street
Minneapolis, Minnesota 55437
(612) 445-9861

EDUCATION   PRINCETON UNIVERSITY, B.A. Economics: 1956

                HARVARD UNIVERSITY, Program for Executives: 1966

EXPERIENCE   REPUBLIC INDUSTRIES
1959-1982   Minneapolis, Minnesota
                Assistant to CEO (1980-1982)

Republic manufactures a variety of transportation industry products for total revenues of $300 million. My position was a holding function until a new acquisition or product line required a general manager. Assignments during these two years included management of a product recall, improvement of product delivery, and transfer of data processing from three sites to one.

REPUBLIC SOFTWARE SERVICES
Vice President, Eastern Region (1976-1980)

Planned, managed, and was P & L responsible for the Eastern regional office of this Republic subsidiary. When the office was closed in 1978, it was profitable with $2 million revenues. The staff of 25 people were conducting studies, designing systems, and operating several computer centers.

REPUBLIC INDUSTRIES
Vice President, Systems (1974-1976)

P & L responsible for the marketing and contract performance of 150 people designing large software systems. This profitable organization, with $10 million revenues, had government and industry as its customer base. Applications included aircraft telemetry systems, insurance policy writing, ships bridge simulator, and telephone company distribution frame inventory.

REPUBLIC INDUSTRIES
Vice President, Operations (1971-1974)

Initial obligation was to mold the people and equipment from seven installations into a single profit making facility. Thereafter managed the $55 million budget of 1500 people and ten computers to service the needs of 500 customers. The services provided included the design of batch, on-line, and real time systems and the operation of IBM, CDC, and Honeywell equipment.

REPUBLIC INDUSTRIES
Assistant to the President (1969-1971)

Participated in the establishment, planning, and growth of this newly formed company.

REPUBLIC AVIATION
Deputy Director, Corporate Planning (1959-1969)

Responsible for the business and technical management section of all proposals for new business, resource management systems, and program planning. This group of 250 people were further responsible for the administration of the corporate budget.

1956-1959   N.C.R.
                 St. Paul, Minnesota
                 Salesman

                 Marketed accounting and microfilm equipment.

OTHER   Who's Who in American Industry and Finance
                 International Biographical Centre, London, England

REFERENCES   On request

John McIntyre
110 North Bay Road
San Francisco, California 94102
(415) 629-5471

EDUCATION: BS, English, University of North Carolina, 1973

                    Intro to Telecommunications, Intro to Microprocessors, Software Configuration Management,
                    IAS Utilities, MACRO-II Assembly Programming, IAS Systems Programming, Application Pro-
                    gramming Operator Training.

CLEARANCE: TOP SECRET CLEARANCE

HARDWARE: IBM 3081, 3082; Honeywell 720, 6080; Intel 8080/85/86; PDP 11/70; Burroughs 3500; Xerox 1200.

SOFTWARE: CP/M 80, 86 IAS RSX-11M, Network Interface, WordStar.

LANGUAGES: 8080/86 Assembler, "C," Macro-II.

PROFESSIONAL
EXPERIENCE:

10/74 to   UNITED STATES NAVY, San Francisco, California
Present   Operations Support Staff: (10/82 to Present) Responsibilities include software development,
                    analysis of software/communication problems, and on-call operational support. Other responsi-
                    bilities include configuration management, technical evaluation of hardware, and software
                    proposals. Also function as a Section Chief and a Trainer.

                    Chief Data Automation Division/Data Processing Manager: (7/81 to 10/82) Responsibilities in-
                    cluded supervising three branches; the interviewing and hiring of civilian personnel, writing
                    job descriptions and the evaluation of personnel. Responsible also for the auditing vendor
                    maintenance forms, executive briefing, contingency planning and resolving data communica-
                    tion problems.

                    Production Control Section/Chief: (7/79 to 7/81) Functioned as a first-line supervisor and was
                    responsible for systems monitor and tape library personnel. Handled all customer complaints,
                    evaluated new data automation requirements and customer education. Equipment control.
                    Also responsible for interviewing, hiring and executive briefing sessions.

                    Computer Operator: (4/77 to 7/79) Responsibilities included operation of operator consoles and
                    all peripherals and remote job entry. Also functioned as a Lead Operator and Shift Supervisor.
                    Responsible for re-creation of tape/disk files, software discrepancy reports and the tape li-
                    brary functions.

                    References upon request.

DOCUMENTATION AND ADMINISTRATIVE SUPPORT

Dorothy Turner
415 Oakes Street
St. Paul, Minnesota 55149
(612) 654-1234

Objective   Secure a position as a technical writer.

Education   M.A. (English), University of Illinois, 1978
                 B.S. (Education), University of Illinois, 1977

Experience   St. Paul High School   1983-84
                 High School English Teacher

                 Responsible for teaching English (writing, grammar,
                 and literature) and history in secondary school.

                 Geigo Terminal Systems, Minneapolis, Minn.   1980-1983
                 Senior Technical Editor (1981-1983)

                 Responsible for editing user manuals, programming
                 guides, and feature summaries for Geigo terminals
                 and related computer equipment.

                 Additionally responsible for the quality control of
                 technical documentation; assisted writers with writing
                 and editing problems, and instructed writers individu-
                 ally and in seminars; also on-call to edit other
                 corporation documents.

                 Instrumental in providing the company with accuracy,
                 precision, and consistency in documentation by re-
                 searching, compiling, and editing a glossary of
                 standard terms used by Geigo in reference to its
                 products. (This glossary and my guidelines for
                 technical writing are still used by Geigo.)

                 Software Technical Writer (1980-1981)

                 Responsible for researching, writing, and producing
                 system operation and programming guides, and feature
                 summaries; assisted in designing the documents from
                 inception through production. Interfaced with
                 engineering, marketing, and graphic arts.

                 Freelance Writer and Consultant   3/79 - 12/81

                 Employed by several computer and publishing firms,
                 as follows:

                 C.B.S. Data Corporation -- Wrote abstracts of
                 articles from commercial banking publications;
                 wrote critiques of competitors' advertising.

                 John Wylie & Sons -- Proofread and copyedited
                 portions of high school texts.

Loeb Publishing -- Wrote exercises for college grammar text; proofread and copyedited the K-8 reading series.

Kodak Corporation -- Edited scientific articles and user manuals.

I.E.E.E. -- Proofread and edited hardware and software documents and textbooks.

Related
Experience

Wrote reviews and feature articles for corporation newspaper; wrote some advertising copy; wrote a critical biography; wrote courses of study.

Conducted workshops and seminars in technical writing and expository composition; chaired committees on curriculum development.

Evaluated compositions for College Entrance Examinations Board.

Taught grammar and writing in college and adult education.

References

On Request.

Judith Cramer
19 Mystic Road
Lancaster, Pennsylvania 17603
(717) 955-4083

CAREER OBJECTIVE

A responsible position as a technical writer/documentation
writer geared toward a potential management position in the
software industry.

EDUCATIONAL BACKGROUND

1978-1979   Penn State (Continuing Education), Scranton, Pa.
             Completed one year
             English/Computer Science

EMPLOYMENT EXPERIENCE

4/82-Present   DOCUMENTATION SPECIALIST
                Virtual Systems, Inc., Lancaster, Pa.
                Responsibilities include writing General Information, User
                and Systems documentation for the Retail Banking Delivery
                Systems (RBDS) used on the IBM 36/4700. RBDS products in-
                clude Automatic Teller Machines (ATMs), Customer Information
                File (CIF), teller terminals, switch and Customer Information
                File interface modules to the ATM Teller System, as well as
                ATM network control features. Established writing standards
                and format and technical reference library. Coordinated
                customer training programs. Ability to read COBOL as well as
                knowledge of ICCF and Vollie command language.

8/81-12/81   ASSOCIATE TECHNICAL WRITER
                Bell Laboratories, Inc., Hershey, Pa.
                Responsibilities included writing test procedures for
                manufactured parts, writing workmanship standards manual,
                writing and implementing company policies and procedures,
                preparing documents for print, maintaining documentation
                library, and establishing technical writing standards.
                Duties also included acting as a liaison among central
                quality, any departments affected by a central quality
                document, and upper management personnel.

EMPLOYMENT EXPERIENCE (Continued)

5/80-10/81   ASSOCIATE TECHNICAL WRITER
               Xerox Corp., New York, N.Y.
               Duties included preparing operator and dealer manuals for
               software applications packages. Researched each software
               application package to obtain an understanding of both
               operator's and dealer's role. Interviewed end-users re-
               garding questions and problems faced when using the soft-
               ware package in order to improve the documentation. Per-
               formed step-by-step instruction of documentation to ensure
               proper functioning of programs and reported any discrepan-
               cies to programmers.

12/76-5/80   EDITORIAL ASSISTANT
               Bradley Co., New York, N.Y.
               Responsibilities included preparing material for audio-
               visual presentation; editing of technical manuals, bro-
               chures, and proposals; and acting as a liaison among cus-
               tomer, writer, and printer. Responsibilities also included
               coordination of manuals, brochures, and proposals. Co-
               ordinated foreign training programs for students.
               Knowledge in the areas of typing, formatting, illustrating,
               photocomposition, audio-visual operations, layout/pasteup,
               printing, reduction percentages and associated specifica-
               tions and standards.

               TECHNICAL TYPIST
               Responsibilities included typing of technical documents
               and proofreading. Involved knowledge of typesetting,
               formatting, and some editing.

SKILLS   Phototypesetting; Kroy Headliner; ITEK 4300 Stat Camera;
               Keypunch; Wang Word Processor; IBM Composer, Teletype;
               36/4700 Teller Terminal. Knowledge of ICCF and Vollie
               commands.

MEMBERSHIPS   National Association for Female Executives (NAFE)
               Society for Technical Communications (STC)

REFERENCES   Available upon request

Elizabeth R. Jonas
3450 Downer Road
Seattle, Washington 98116

Telephone: (206) 576-8934
(206) 570-1200

EDUCATION

M.B.A., Management - Graduate School of Business Administration, New York University, New York, New York: June 1968.

B.A., History, Rochester University, New York: February 1953.

Experience
1982 -
Present

Oakland Electronics Corporation, Seattle, Washington

TECHNICAL PUBLICATIONS MANAGER
Manage a department of technical publication specialists responsible for publishing CAD/CAM hardware and software user documents. Provide writing, editing, data entry, and technical art services. Hire and train personnel. Plan and schedule new product documentation. Work directly with management and engineering. Conduct technical reviews and field testing of technical publications.
Accomplishments include: organizing the new department, writing job descriptions and hiring personnel, work flow, job scheduling, technical review, and document update procedures. Instituted reader response card, glossary of graphics technical terms, on-line library, and CADAM generated technical articles. Published internal documentation standards and procedures, and implemented a computerized (VAX/VMS) system for editing, formatting, file transfer, and document maintenance.

1980-1982

Arthur Andersen & Co., Washington, D.C.

SOFTWARE DOCUMENTATION PRODUCTION MANAGER
Directed 12-15 publications production specialists responsible for publishing 20-30 software user documents of 200-500 pages per year. Managed the daily operation of the department, which included supervisors for design, data entry, technical art, and proofreading. Participated with management in planning and developing new software products. Prepared and administered annual budgets, and purchased supplies, equipment, and outside services.
Accomplishments included: expanding the group's services to include design and production of handbooks, pocket guides, and newsletters. Implemented a DEC, TMS-11 computer-based text management and phototypesetting system requiring the hiring, cross-training, and re-assigning of personnel.

1978-1980   Computer Systems of America, Atlanta, Ga.

             SUPERVISOR OF PUBLICATIONS PRODUCTION
             Headed a group of seven, responsible for producing the
             company's advertising, promotional, marketing, and tech-
             nical publications. Services included phototypesetting,
             creative brochure design, product photography, trade show
             exhibits, and sales presentations. Contracted with out-
             side vendors for creative art, photography, and printing.
             Attended a comprehensive management training program,
             emphasizing corporate planning, goal setting, and manage-
             ment by objectives.

1976-1978   Georgia State Department of Engineering, Atlanta, Ga.

             SUPERVISOR OF DRAFTING AND DOCUMENTATION
             Supervised the design and production of all publications,
             including civil engineering reports, land use and popula-
             tion studies, statistical reports, etc. Hired the staff,
             purchased equipment, and established procedures (complying
             with Government standards) to meet state publication
             requirements. Interfaced with other State agencies,
             sharing information and resources. Set up a training pro-
             gram with the local CETA office to train the unemployed in
             a variety of graphic arts skills.

1973-1976   Allison Associates, Atlanta, Ga.

             DESIGN DIRECTOR
             Directed a group of 24 book designers, reprint editors,
             and phone editors. Responsibilities included hiring,
             training, assigning and scheduling tasks, budgeting,
             quality control, and planning new projects. Participated
             in the launching of a reading program setting new standards
             of quality for the art and design of elementary readers.

1970-1973   Waverly Computers, Atlanta, Ga.

             COMMERCIAL PUBLICATIONS ILLUSTRATOR AND DESIGNER
             Established an art and design group to service the newly
             formed commercial printing and publishing department. Met
             with clients to discuss their publications requirements,
             developed budgets and scheduled jobs through production.
             Participated in a government program (Manpower Training Act)
             to train inner city residents in graphic arts skills.

Member of Art Director's Club of Seattle, Bookbuilders of Atlanta, National
Association of Industrial Artists, Society of Technical Communicators,
Watercolor Society.

References furnished.

Barbara Berkman
47 East 72nd Street
New York, New York 10027

OBJECTIVE	Technical Writer

PROFESSIONAL
ACCOMPLISHMENTS

Software

. Designed and implemented programs in BASIC,
  ASSEMBLY, and COBOL
. Logged 200+ hours on the DEC PDP-11/44
. Created text files and source programs
  using EMACS
. Completed course on Wang word processor

Writing

. Completed 200 hours of technical writing
  instruction
. Wrote technical documents:
  - JCL Reference Manual
  - EMACS Reference Guide
. Designed instructional materials including:
  - 3 videocassette training aids for
    welfare workers
  - course syllabus with 30 content units
  - more than 30 course handouts
  - 2 chapters of an instructional booklet
  - evaluation questionnaires

Training

. Prepared and delivered training program to
  clerical staff of NY State Welfare Department
. Designed and delivered classroom lectures
. Trained and supervised instructional staff
  of 15
. Utilized a wide variety of audiovisual equipment including films, slides, overheads,
  videocassettes, and slide tapes
. Performed needs analyses and implemented
  programs based on results of analyses

Management

. Acted as department coordinator; supervised
  faculty
. Interviewed, evaluated, and recommended candidates for university faculty positions
. Negotiated learner contracts at community
  agencies
. Chaired Course Development Committee
. Coordinated social services to a diverse
  community population

EDUCATION
- Technical Writing Program, Brooklyn Community College, 1984
- Personnel Development: Design of Training Programs, Hofstra University, 1981
- M.S. in Social Work, Hofstra University, 1980, GPA 3.9
- B.S. in English, SUNY, Stony Brook, 1968, Magna Cum Laude

EXPERIENCE
- Staff Social Worker. St. Joseph's Hospital, Long Island, N.Y. 1981-1983
- Instructor, Parent Education. St. Joseph's Hospital, Long Island, N.Y. 1978-1983
- Assistant Professor, School of Social Services. Long Island University, 1975-1981
- Social Worker, N.Y. State Social Services Program, New York, New York. 1970-1974
- Social Worker, St. Joseph's Hospital, Long Island, N.Y. 1968-1970

PROFESSIONAL
ORGANIZATION

Society for Technical Communication

REFERENCES

References and writing sample available upon request

RICHARD A. REESE
48 Cass Ave.
Falls Church, Va. 22040
(703) 947-6121

JOB OBJECTIVE

To research, write, and edit marketing literature in support of a proprietary product or company publication.

EDUCATION

B.A. English, University of Texas, Austin, Tx., 1980.
Minor: History.

Completed "Introduction to Data Processing" course at Baltimore Community College, June 1983.

PROFESSIONAL EXPERIENCE

1980 -   OMEGA SYSTEMS INCORPORATED, Reston, Va.
present   Promotional Writer
               Editing and writing of promotional and technical ma-
               terials in support of GENERAL SOFTWARE, OSI Program
               Products' proprietary software product. Accomplish-
               ments include:

               - Researching, writing, and editing a 35-page GENERAL
                 SOFTWARE Information Manual for use in providing
                 clients with information of both a sales and techni-
                 cal nature.

               - Writing and editing news and feature stories for OSI
                 Program Products' company newsletter. Contributed
                 to the initial layout, design, photography, and
                 coordination of final printing.

               - Writing and editing news articles for the GENERAL
                 SOFTWARE National User Group Newsletter.

               - Editing various marketing/sales brochures, including
                 seminar handouts, scripts for media production, and
                 inserts to existing brochures.

               - Reorganization and rewriting the GENERAL SOFTWARE
                 user documentation consisting of fifteen independent
                 manuals.

               Control, price, stock, print, and distribute all GENERAL
               SOFTWARE technical documentation, which includes user
               manuals, installation manuals, and training tutorials.

Richard A. Reese
Page Two

RELATED EXPERIENCE

- Edited law briefs for correct grammar and style while working in a Washington, D.C. law firm. Summer 1978.

- Compiled research questionnaire for undergraduate English majors. 1979-80.

- Wrote Zeta Beta Tau fraternity factsheet flyer to be distributed during freshman rush. 1979.

- Compiled photo-journalistic scrapbook covering two-month period of study/travel in Paris, France. Summer 1979.

- Composed photo-essay book on skydiving for photography class. Spring 1981.

ACTIVITIES AND HONORS

Zeta Beta Tau fraternity - Executive Coordinator, 1980-81; Activities Chairman, 1979-80; Chaplain, 1980-81; Election Chairman, 1981.
Undergraduate English Club - Secretary, 1979-80.
Accepted for summer school program at the Sorbonne, Paris, France. Summer, 1979.

INTERESTS

Nationally ranked runner, photography, sailing.

REFERENCES and WRITING SAMPLES available upon request.

```
                        Betty Jo Kim
                        46 Pollack Ave.
                      Albany, N.Y. 12201


Objective:     A position as proofreader/editor of technical,
               statistical, engineering, marketing, and training
               manuals leading to senior editor or manager of
               proofreading.

Education:     Troy Junior College   Troy, N.Y.   Associate Degree/
                                                  Advertising

Experience:    Information Systems Distributors   Albany, N.Y.
               1980-1982
               Senior Proofreader/Word Processor

               •  Developed and implemented proofreading,
                  formatting, and documentation procedures
                  and standards for customer specifications
                  and internal departmental use.

               •  Supervised and trained proofreaders to
                  facilitate document processing and pro-
                  duction.

               •  Assisted technical writers in editing and
                  formatting all hardware and software
                  manuals, including proofreading and editing
                  of a baseline specification supporting com-
                  puter-based distribution systems for Fortune
                  1000 Companies.

               •  Consulted and coordinated with authors and
                  contract/project managers to meet deadlines
                  and deliver quality documents.

               •  Proficient in advanced features of the WORD-
                  11 word processing system.

               Federal Trade Commission   Albany, N.Y.
               1979-1980
               Department Coordinator of Word Processing

               •  Implemented office procedures and determined
                  optimal applications using a Lanier word pro-
                  cessing system at the regional headquarters.

               •  Responsible for all phases of document processing
                  and production under the direction of the chief,
                  Management Systems Division.
```

- Reviewed all incoming material, coordinated document processing to ensure that deadlines were met,
  and quality controlled finished product.

- Interfaced with department heads to ensure efficient utilization of the system resources.

- Responsible for the training and supervision of
  word processing operators as well as being the
  liaison between internal division users and external divisions when required.

Albany Community Hospital   Albany, N.Y.
1976-1979
Medical Records Assistant

- Assisted in daily operations of the Medical
  Records and Billing Departments as well as
  the Business Office including filing, quality
  control of official documents, and occasional
  clerical duties.

References available upon request

Barbara Winters
1645 West Brook Drive
Cambridge, MA 02157
(617) 455-6767
(617) 521-4621

EDUCATION

Emanual College, Boston, MA

Bachelor of Science in Management. Concentration:
Management Information Systems. Expected Graduation
Date: May, 1984

PROFESSIONAL COURSEWORK

IBM DCF for Text Administrators and Programmers
MODEL 204 DBMS User Language Course
MODEL 204 DBMS File Manager Course

BUSINESS EXPERIENCE

John F. Forbes & Co., Cambridge, MA
(1980 to Present)

Manage IBM Text Processing Section of the Text Processing Department
in Publications Division. Coordinate text processing production of
commercial documentation. Develop standards and procedures for text
data entry, and systems and procedures for interface with writers.
Periodic written communications concerning policies, procedures, and
technical information to text processing and documentation personnel.
Currently involved in major project to put user manual set for major
software product (Database Management System) online.

Developed a course on the use of the editor (Xedit) and text formatting
program (Script). Teach all classes of users utilizing foils and handouts.

Modified text processing software (text programming) to conform to corporate documentation standards. Ongoing written documentation of all
changes to that software.

Coordination of hardware and software interface from IBM System 370
computer system to Compugraphic 8400 typesetter. This effort involves
coordinating the efforts of systems programming, operations, text processing, and graphics personnel; and research into existing computerized
software interfaces.

Brown Associates, Boston, MA
(1978-1980)

Mastered sophisticated typesetting techniques with the aid of various
equipment including a state-of-the-art, computerized typesetting system.

Wrote training manual for data entry personnel. Clients included
Boston Magazine, Boston Edison, Teaching Resources, Little Brown,
Allyn and Bacon, and Instrumentation Laboratories.

Emanual College/School of Education, Boston, MA
(November 1976 - February 1978)

Coordinated work flow from 12 departments, pre-approved transfer
credits, supervised work/study personnel, trained new personnel,
designed forms, organized and implemented special projects.

Emanual College/Registrar's Office, Boston, MA
(June 1975 - November 1977)

Researched and solved problems related to transcripts and trained
new personnel. Interacted extensively with students, other departments, and lending institutions.

Business Mail Order List Service, Inc., Boston, MA
(August 1973 - June 1975)

Compiled demographic lists, processed mail, and initiated efficient
reorganization of sample inserts.

PERSONAL

Hobbies: Sailing, Reading, Chess

Willing to relocate

References on request

Lori Miles
43 Sunburst Rd
Atlanta, Ga. 30303
(404) 447-2156

EDUCATION

1978-1979   Katharine Gibbs School, Atlanta, Ga.
             Course: Liberal Arts-Administrative Program
             Honor Roll

1975-1978   Rosewood High School, Atlanta, Ga.
             Course: Business

CLEARANCE   DEFENSE DEPARTMENT SECRET

EXPERIENCE

1979-Present KILGORE, KING AND REYNOLDS, INC., Atlanta, Ga.
             Position: Staff Assistant

             Responsibilities: Secretary to the Director of Contracts
             and the government contracts department at KKR Communica-
             tions Corporation. This involves maintaining the director's
             calendar, preparing reports and proposals, administering
             budgets, preparing budgetary estimates for contracts,
             coordinating itineraries, interacting with government and
             commercial clients, and handling of classified material.

             The position requires use of applications programs on
             DEC PDP-10, PDP-20, and PDP-11 computers and on KKR's
             X/40 computer system. These programs include the PEN,
             EMACs, and TECO text editors; the HERMES and MSG electronic
             mail systems; and the VISICALC ledger sheet program. In
             addition to running applications on stand-alone computers,
             I am familiar with procedures to access remote applications
             and data bases using packet switching networks. These
             procedures include the ARPANET File Transfer-Protocol and
             TELENET Protocol.

             Previous position at KKR was as assistant to the head of
             the Systems Analysis Department.

             Responsibilities: preparation of reports and preparation
             of camera-ready copies of journal articles; also super-
             vision of document preparation. Served as assistant to
             the editor of the Computer Communications Review and was
             responsible in the preparation of each issue. Administra-
             tive responsibilities to the technical staff also included
             handling personnel records on monies, travel, and expenses,
             arranging company/client-oriented luncheons and conferences,
             and transmitting worldwide TELEX and TWX messages

Lori Miles, page 2

1975-1979   MEDICAL SYSTEMS, INC., Atlanta, Ga.
               Position: Secretary-receptionist

               Duties: Typing, receiving and greeting patients, filing,
               billing, part-time lab technician, home visits and nursing
               home visits, on-call weekend technician duties, operating
               emergency testing equipment.

SKILLS

Knowledge of several computer text editing, text formatting, and
electronic mail programs which run under the UNIX, TENEX, TOPS-20, and
RSX-11 operating systems. Knowledge of bookkeeping techniques and
facility with VisiCalc. Knowledge of lab technology, hematology,
medical terminology and third-party billing. Typing and filing skills.
Knowledge of Italian.

REFERENCES

Available upon request.

CONSTANCE ANITA KRAVITZ
456 Philadelphia Road
Camden, NJ 08705

EDUCATION

1972 - 1973:   Attended Johnson & Wales College
Providence, Rhode Island

1972:   Graduated, Taunton High School
Taunton, Massachusetts
Academic/Business Course

SPECIALIZED TRAINING

1982   Model 204 Basic User Language Course
1983   IBM Script Training Course
1983   EMACS Editor Course

EXPERIENCE

March 1981 -
Present

COMPUTER PRODUCTS OF AMERICA
Philadelphia, PA

Assistant to V.P. Sales, Commercial Products

Coordinate and organize all sales-related activities,
including seminars, lead tracking system, brochures,
and communications. Coordinate activites and scheduling for 15 branch office sales and support personnel.
Manage activities of 2 assistants; provide information
to customers and prospects.

July 1979 -
March 1981

NORTHEAST SOLAR ENERGY CENTER
Boston, MA

Senior Secretary, Purchasing Department

Responsibilities include organizing, initiating, and
monitoring purchasing system; coordinating all purchasing activities for a company with a $9 million
annual budget (i.e., directing support staff, ordering supplies and equipment, and working closely with
manager). Possess in-house expertise with Rolm CBX
Telephone System and Data Base Management of system.

November 1975 -
July 1979

FIRST DISTRICT COURT OF BRISTOL
Taunton, MA 02780

Secretary to Presiding Justice

Special responsibilities included full-time Acting
Clerk of Six-Man Jury Session (January 1, 1979 -
July 1979); Session's Clerk, District Court main

session; caseflow management clerk; and Budget
Coordinator of the Court. Budgetary responsibilities included being called upon by the Supreme
Judicial Court in Boston to lecture at numerous
conferences and seminars regarding budgetary preparation and submission.

June 1971 -   MARTIN AND STROJNY, ATTORNEYS
November 1975   Taunton, MA

Legal Secretary

Trained in all aspects of real estate/probate
practice both as paralegal and secretary.

June 1976 to   REHOBOTH POLICE DEPARTMENT
1978   Rehoboth, MA

Dispatcher

Responsible for the quick and efficient dispatching
of all police, fire, and rescue vehicles and personnel. Duties also included answering all routine
and emergency telephone calls, daily log upkeep,
accident reports, and police reports.

ACADEMIC HONORS

1972 Rhode Island Invitational Business Skills Meet
Sponsored by Johnson & Wales College
Providence, RI

Tri-State Champion of Massachusetts,
Connecticut, and Rhode Island
1st Prize: $1,600 Full Tuition Scholarship
          to Johnson & Wales College

References upon request

TECHNICAL SUPPORT PERSONNEL

RAYMOND W. CLANCY   •   6518 Grant Place   •   West New York, NJ 07093   •   (201) 867-7777

EDUCATION: New York University, New York, NY; B.S. in Computer Science, 1975

IBM Classes attended:

- Data Base Organization and Control
- DBOMP Implementation and Programming
- COBOL/File Handling Techniques
- DOS/VS System Implementation
- VSAM Coding
- VM/370 Installation
- VM/370 Problem Source Identification
- VM/370 for Systems Programmers
- VSE System Advanced Topics
- CICS/VS Installation and System Generation
- CICS/VS Recovery and Restart

HARDWARE & SOFTWARE: IBM 3031, 4341, 370s, 3705-EP, VM/SP, CMS, IPF, OS/VS1, DOS/VSE, DOS/VS, CICS/VS, WEST I, BTAM, VSAM, POWER/VS, BAL, COBOL, FORTRAN, PANVALET, EPAT, WEST I, CULPRIT, EDGAR, Honeywell 6000.

EXPERIENCE:
September 1979 to Present

COMPUTER INTERNATIONAL CO., INC.
West New York, NJ

SENIOR SYSTEMS SOFTWARE PROGRAMMER

Install, maintain, and tune VM, DOS/VS-E, DOS/VS. Install CICS. Train junior software programmers as well as the programming and operations staff. Develop productivity aids and evaluate packages. Installed:

- VM/SP, SEPP, (rel 1.2)
- VM/SP, BSEP, (rel 1.1)
- VM/370, SCP, (rel 6.18)
- DOS/VSE (rel 3)
- CICS/VS (rel 1.5)
- DOS/VS (rel 34.14)
- Packages such as ISP and IPF, CPWATCH, DYNAMT
- Waterloo modification

Developed and/or modified software in-house:

- Tape Management System under VM/SP used for automatic Backup (IPL' able) of VM/SP environment. IPF (5748-MS1) procedures and panels modified to provide a nondestructive user-initiated restore of any/all CMS files.
- DOS/VS and VSE Library update audit using a VM service virtual machine and VMCF.
- Modification of CMS PSERV program (DMSPRV) to see private procedure libraries.

December
1975 to
September
1979

S.D. ANDREWS, INC.
Scranton, PA

SENIOR SOFTWARE ANALYST (1/78 to 9/79)

Responsible for the installation, system generation, and maintenance of VM/370 at 6.5 level. Installation of all packages under VM include: COBOL/VS, OS PL/1, APL, FORTRAN, VS BASIC, DMS, EDGAR, EP/VS, IIS, CMS, Direct Maintenance PP, VMAP.

In addition, installed and maintained DOS/VS at rel. 34.14 AF1. Packages include: COBOL/VS, EPAT/VS, PANVALET, WESTI, Westinghouse Disk Dump/Restore, FORTRAN IV Option 1 and Library, and CULPRIT.

Conversion of DOS/VS environment off Corporate Computer (3031) to subsidiary's computer (370/145). All production problems on OS/VSI system—any and all JCL problems and assisted in package installation.

LEAD SOFTWARE ANALYST (9/75 to 12/77)

Responsible for the conversion of DOS/VS environment from subsidiary's computer (370/135) to Corporate computer (370/148). Upgraded DOS/VS from rel 32 to rel 34.14 AF1. Trained operators in operation of DOS/VS under VM/370. Trained software personnel in maintenance of DOS/VS.

Installed VM/370 on Corporate computer (370/148) and established procedure for review and acceptance of in-house modifications to any Corporate Operating System. Installation and system generation of OS/VS1 under VM/370.

REFERENCES: On request

Jose L. Hernandez   R.D. 143 Framingham, Massachusetts 01701   966-4985

OBJECTIVE: A systems programming position in business/commercial or engineering systems.

EDUCATION: **BRANDEIS UNIVERSITY**
9/79-Present   Special Graduate Student

                       Coursework in Knowledge Based Application Systems, and currently enrolled in Data Base Management Systems.

9/72-6/76   **BRANDEIS UNIVERSITY**
                       BS in Computer Science and Engineering

EXPERIENCE: **GCC SYSTEMS, Waltham, Massachusetts**
1981-1984   Systems Programmer

                       Responsible for new programs and maintenance tasks on DECsystem-10 (TOPS-10), Univac 494, and VAX-11/780 computers, using assembly languages (MACRO-10, SPURT, and VAX-11 MACRO), Pascal, and FORTRAN. Tasks included:

* KRGLIB, a utility for transferring, translating, and reformatting file in the GCC Report Generator II programming language.
* DECUS Pascal compiler and run-time library enhancements.
* DISKTEST enhancements to simulate random access of disk storage.
* TIM2 modification to an 8080 microprocessor controlled terminal.
* Maintenance of two macro libraries for generating COBOL data descriptions.
* PDT, a resident PDP-11/10 debugger for Remote Message Concentrators.

1972-1981   **RAYTHEON DATA SYSTEMS, Wilmington, Massachusetts**
                       Member of the Technical Staff
                       Developed extensions and enhancements to USAF-owned Computer Assisted Design Specification and Analysis Tool (CADSAT), programmed in PL/I and FORTRAN. Performed requirements analysis for USAF Joint Surveillance System project, a radar and computer-based air defense network, and later performed design-to-requirements analysis of Boeing Aircraft design documentation. Participated in preparation and submission of proposals.

MILITARY:
9/79-Present

AIR FORCE RESERVES
Communications - Electronics Platoon Leader

Completed Signal Officers Advanced Course in 1979. Current rank of First Lieutenant.

<u>1034 USAR SCHOOL</u>
Instructor

Taught MOS classes in Radio-Telephone.

References upon request.

Alice Hawkins
465 West End Avenue
New York, New York 10023
(212) 622-4802

OBJECTIVE: Position as a data base training and education specialist

EDUCATION: COLUMBIA UNIVERSITY. 1978
                  B.S. Chemistry.

                  Scatlin Continuing Education
                  Data Base Development   Reporting Internals and Efficiencies
                  File/Terminal Driven Maintenance   Advanced Analytical Techniques

TECHNICAL   IBM 370, 4300, 303X, (VP CSS), Prime 750 (PRIMOS), PDP-11 (RSTS/E), Honeywell Level 62
BACKGROUND: (GCOS).

                  COBOL, FORTRAN, BASIC.

                  HIGHLITE II.

PROFESSIONAL   SCATLIN ELECTRONICS, New York, New York
EXPERIENCE:
3/81-Present   SENIOR TECHNICAL REPRESENTATIVE
                  Scatlin is a time-sharing service company. Their primary product is a 4th-generation, relational
                  data base management system called HIGHLITE. HIGHLITE is a combination DBMS end-user
                  reporting system and higher level language, complete with extended capabilities in graphics,
                  statistical analysis, and decision support. My work in the Information Center primarily involves
                  providing technical support and training to users of HIGHLITE, as well as Software, Marketing,
                  and Training and Education as detailed below:

                  Software Support:

                  * Design applications software utilizing HIGHLITE for customers in a variety of areas
                     including health care, demographics, financial planning, cost analysis, etc. This includes
                     defining requirements with the user, doing a schematic, setting up and loading the data
                     base, implementing procedures for reports, etc.
                  * Analyze and solve customer application problems on-site or by telephone.
                  * Provide ongoing technical support to internal personnel and end-users in an on-line time-
                     sharing network.

                  Marketing Support:

                  * Prepare and deliver technical presentations, the largest one being a demonstration for the
                     U.S. Transportation Office involving 600,000 records.
                  * Accompany marketing representatives on prospective sales calls 3 to 6 times per month.

                  Training and Education Support:

                  * Teach standardized courses on: Data Base Design; Maintenance and Reporting; Financial
                     Analysis Software; Operating System Introduction (VP CSS, modified IBM OS/CMS);
                     Executive Command Language; Proprietary, 3rd Party Software.

                  Certified in a 3-month program to teach Advanced Data Base classes. Tested by corporate
                  office on both product knowledge and presentation skill. Also coordinate branch education
                  program and develop nonstandard courses.

5/78 - 3/81   MULTIPLE ACCESS, INC., New York, New York

SENIOR PROGRAMMER ANALYST

Managed the development of an on-line internal accounting system for MIS. Participated in the design of Order/Entry and Production Control systems; both on-line.

Designed and programmed interactive, user-oriented inquiry systems. Coding done in COBOL.

Implemented text processing and word processing system to meet client specifications.

Involved heavily in the conversion of all production systems from the DEC PDP-11 to a Prime 750. Coding done in COBOL.

References on request.

Cheryl Newman
1231 Orchid Street
Los Angeles, California 90068
Phone: (213) 989-2406

OBJECTIVE: A position that will allow me to utilize both my teaching and customer interface skills.

EDUCATION: University of California, Los Angeles
Course work in Computer Science

California State College, Long Beach
Liberal Arts; 1980

HARDWARE: IBM 3033, 370/168, Amdahl V8

LANGUAGES: NOMAD, COBOL, BASIC, FORTRAN

EXPERIENCE: SCIENTIFIC PROGRAMMING INC., Los Angeles, California
Education Specialist   12/82 - Present

Instructor for Scientific Development Systems/On-line. Teaches on-line Development Language for maintaining an IDMS database or VSAM file using screen formatted programs.

NATIONAL TRAINING SYSTEMS, INC., Los Angeles, California
Senior Technical Representative   6/80 - 12/82

* Provide on-going technical training to customers in analysis, development, and enhancement of commercial applications (including inventory, financial modeling, spread sheets, budgeting and accounting systems).

* Design and implement customer and internal applications utilizing database management systems.

* Develop financial models for MIS including budgeting, cash flow/forecast analysis and revenue forecasting utilizing internationally developed financial software in conjunction with fourth-generation database tools.

Training and Education

* Coordinate branch education program.

* Train new technical personnel in support, teaching techniques, and system efficiencies.

* Develop and instruct nonstandardized courses for customers and internal staff.

(over)

EXPERIENCE: (Con't.)

* Teach standardized courses including: database design, maintenance and reporting; financial analysis software; introduction to the operating system.

Branch Office Administrator   5/79 - 6/80

* Coordinate office efforts in major sales activities.

* Assist customers in definition and correction of software application problems.

* Design and develop online DBMS applications and standardized reporting procedures to conform with company reporting requirements.

* Assist specialists in the installation of additional network equipment; also assist in application of remedial measures to correct failure of same.

* Document standard and emergency procedures for operation of branch hardware and office procedures.

References upon request

JEREMY GIBBONS
186 Intracoastal Highway
Boca Raton, Florida 33448
(305) 965-9328

OBJECTIVE　　To participate in a creative team effort to support software for online systems and for datacommunications.

PROGRAMMING SKILLS

—COBOL, IBM ASSEMBLER, FORTRAN, PASCAL, BASIC
Currently in Study Group learning ADA

—IBM, JCL, HIS JCL, IBM Dump Reading, HIS Dump Reading

—TSO, TSO/SPF, PANVALET, HIS TSS, ATS, CMS

—ATMS, EASYTRIEVE, ADRS2BG, AUTOTAB

—VSAM, ISAM, IMS, IDS

—CICS, DMS, BMS, EDF, DMSDBUG, INTEREST

EMPLOYMENT HISTORY

**Feb. 1981-
Present**　　**Westinghouse Elevator, Miami, Fla. 33110**
Responsible for supporting CICS, DMS, and BMS. Duties include: overseeing design of application systems using VSAM, IMS, and ISAM; providing technical support to applications programmers; testing and approving/rejecting migration of application system from test to production; providing training materials; developing debugging techniques using EDF, DMSDBUG, and INTEREST; generating CICS Tables; reviewing and testing vendor software to aid online development; etc.

Trained in Datacommunications on the job and by attending seminars by Technology Concepts, Inc.

**Jan. 1978-
Feb. 1981**　　**Associated Hospital Services, Inc., Miami, Fla. 33120**
Combination Programmer and Data Processing Trainer for the Computer Operations Area. Batch programming for records management and hardware/software problem tracking. Designed and taught data processing courses. Responsible for project on history of computing at the company.

EDUCATION

1976   MA in History and Philosophy of Science, University of New Mexico.

1974   BA, summa cum laude and Phi Beta Kappa, in Philosophy (emphasis on Philosophy of Science), University of New Hampshire.

PROFESSIONAL ORGANIZATIONS
National Member of ACM
Member of Miami Computer Society

TECHNICAL WRITING
Experience in writing Systems Documentation, Benchmark Reports, and Technical Support Guides (1982)

Experience in writing Programmer's Guides and User's Guides for Application Systems (1978-1982)

Experience in designing and writing Data Processing Training Courses (1978-1980)

REFERENCES   On Request

Gregory L. Charleston
78 Oaktree Drive
Philadelphia, Pa. 19012
(215) 547-9834

EDUCATION   TEMPLE UNIVERSITY, Philadelphia, Pa.
BA in Mathematics, 1969

HARDWARE   Amdahl 470/V6 F8
IBM 360 40/50/65/75 370 145/3031/3033 4341 3850 3705 2250 S/7 1401 7094
Interdata (Perkin-Elmer) 5 50 70

SOFTWARE   MVS/SP, OS/VSI, OS/MVT, SVS, VM/370/SP, DOS/VSE,
EXPERIENCE   DOS/MVT/VSE CICS/VS, VSAM
TSO, SPF, TONE, CMS, CONDOR
PANVALET, EASYTRIEVE, HSM, QED, FSE, SCRIPT, SMP, MVS CLISTS
PL/1, BAL COBOL, Fortran, MAC, APL, Autocoder
All areas of OS/VS data management, including EXCP
Extensive graphics experience using various software/hardware

EXPERIENCE: MONASH LABORATORIES, INC. Philadelphia, Pa.
Senior Consultant   July 1982-present

Function as both Management and Technical Consultant to clients in the insurance, manufacturing, software development, and services industries. Involved in operational optimization; hardware and software planning, selection, installation, and training; ongoing technical and application support and development. Technical educational courses developed and taught for several clients.

PURITAN LABORATORIES. Allentown, Pa.
Computation Service Manager   May 1977-June 1982

Responsible for operations of the internal computer service bureau used by most engineering projects at the Laboratory. Organized into Operations, System Software, and User Services Sections, the Computation Services Division runs a large IBM-compatible facility including an Amdahl 470/V8 running MVS/SE2 with TSO, IBM 4341 running VM/SP/CMS, and large complement of peripherals including 3270s, various start/stop and BSC lines, a dozen RJE stations around the country, 2 3800 laser printers, 3850 mass storage system (MSS), 52 3350s, etc.

Management responsibilities include hiring, appraisal, salary review, staff development, and technical direction of about 30 people, including tracking of both routine operations and longer-term projects. Responsible for technical support of entire installation. Technical involvements have included studies of new software and hardware, consultation with staff on plans and new facilities, design of system usability improvements, and performance measurement and capacity planning.

Management responsibility for installation upgrades, including MVS conversion and MSS installation. Installation of an IBM 3850 MSS in 1980 achieved full production without ANY disruption of the existing workload.

Final activities included responsibility for upgrade of MSS hardware, conversion to ACF2 security software, planning operations of recently installed 4341 VM/CMS system, and planning new software including graphics and text processing.

UNIVERSITY OF PENNSYLVANIA, Pa.
System Programmer   July 1974-April 1977

Technical support for IBM system software including MVT, SVS, and VM. Installation of first 3350 disks in area. Installed VM/370. Technical work on conversion from MVT to SVS. Programming assistance to other computer users. Extensive work in data management area: improved reliability of in-house-developed data migration system; made modifications to IEHMOVE, linkage editor, FDR; developed volume compaction software; investigated mass storage alternatives. Configured IBM 3850 MSS, planned installation and conversion.

Other technical involvements: modifications of IBM 3705 software to support nonstandard plotter and graphical devices; performance measurement and bench-marking, and measurement of operating systems running under VM; IBM System/7-based data acquisition and transmission system used for remote data processing during engineering field test; software for computer-to-computer link for use in real-time hybrid simulations. Acted as internal consultant in areas such as investigation of new hardware and software, system analysis of user requirements, and as part of specification language processor design group. Member of minicomputer acquisition review team.

MARKS CLINIC FOUNDATION, Dallas, Tex.
Project and Technical Support Leader   August 1969-June 1974

Headed five-person applications development group. Hiring, review, systems analysis for medical applications, program specifications, supervision of program development. Installed enhancements to online patient appointment scheduling system. After CICS technical education, planned conversion of scheduling system to OS CICS. Designed revenue reporting system. Designed billing system and led development work to installation. Designed library control system to audit program libraries. Continued technical role, providing all installation's technical support. Trained and supervised a system programming successor.

REFERENCES   On request

MICHAEL M. DANKO
1233 Ravan Park Avenue
White Plains, New York 10625
(914) 332-2277

Education	M.B.A. program (1973), University of Kentucky; 27 hours of business prerequisites and 9 hours of graduate work
	New York University, M.A.; 1972
	St. Louis University, A.B. magna cum laude; 1970
Professional Experience 1978 - present	BANKER'S TRUST CO., New York, New York

Professional
Experience
1978 - present   BANKER'S TRUST CO., New York, New York

Position: Manager, Timesharing Services (2/81 to Present)

Supervision of a group of 6 people with responsibility for technical support and user interface for in-house timesharing systems (600 users); coordination of the use of outside timesharing services (500 users). Timesharing billing, and the provision of consulting services in various applications to the timesharing community. Now working on a 2-year plan for consolidation of all time sharing on a dedicated in-house system.

Position: Manager Software Products (1978 to 1981)

Supervision of a group of 9 people with responsibility for the implementation and maintenance of an interactive programming development system using VM/CMS, installation and support of user-related program products (compilers, utilities, etc.), technical support for all applications groups within Banker's Trust, and installation and support of TI and DEC software. Had major project responsibility for the VM/CMS system from planning to implementation; project completed on time and within budget.

(continued on page 2)

1974 to 1978   WESTERN UNION, St. Louis, Missouri

Position: Senior Systems Analyst

Responsible for all computing: 2 major systems, computer-assisted instruction, research projects, and hardware and software planning. Supervised 5 people.

1973-1974   XTRA CORPORATION, Chicago, Illinois

Position: Standards and Education Manager

Responsible for standards and education of all applications programming groups and for evaluation and selection of software packages.

REFERENCES FURNISHED UPON REQUEST

Sharon Cook Darrow
65 Elm Street
Kirkwood, Mo. 63122

Telephone: (314) 653-2244

EDUCATION: B.S. Accounting, Columbia University, 1972

                Class rank: 3/500. Grade point: 3.8/4.0

OBJECTIVE: To participate in the design, development, and implementation of major applications systems
                utilizing Database Technology

HARDWARE: IBM 3033, 3081, 4331, 370. IBM P.C., H.P. 3000, Z80, 8088

SOFTWARE: OS/MVS, VM, VS1, CMS, IDMS, IDMS/DC, ADS-ON LINE, OLM, IDD, Culprit, Wylbur/Interact,
                QLQ

LANGUAGE: (HEAVY) IBM Assembler, COBOL, ADS/0

EMPLOYMENT: ATLANTIC SOFTWARE, Kirkwood, Mo. 63120
4/80 - Present Post Sales Technical Support Specialist

                Provide customers with the technical information and guidance necessary to enable the
                successful *implementation* and ongoing use of Atlantic's system software product line.

                Technical Support demands an in-depth knowledge of the internals of database systems,
                data dictionaries, teleprocessing monitors, and all of the components which make up the
                IBM mainframe environment. Additionally, the ability to communicate with customers having
                a wide range of data processing backgrounds is essential for this position.

2/76-4/80   HUDSON DATA, INC., Scranton, Pa. 18520
                Applications Programmer

                Consulted with and provided programming services to project teams organized to satisfy the
                customized data processing needs of company's clients.

                This position required proficiency in Fortran, *IBM 370 Assembly* language and in the use of
                company's database management software.

9/72-1/76   PACIFIC TRACKING CO., Boston, Mass. 02153
                Marketing Manager

                Conceptualized and executed two very successful retail marketing campaigns. Based on this
                accomplishment, I was asked to develop the start-up plan for a manufacturer interested in
                supplying the markets in which my company was doing business.

ASSOCIATIONS: Director of the Database Users Group, Atlantic Computer Society

References on request

CARLETON K. ROBERTS ● 16 Bell Street ● Harris, Minnesota 55941

Telephone: 218-583-9313 (home)   218-518-8000 (work)

OBJECTIVE: Position in customer support, training, project management, or programming

EDUCATION: UNIVERSITY OF PENNSYLVANIA, 1972-1976

B.A. in Psychology. Minor in German and Sociology.

Academic Honors: Phi Beta Kappa Honor Society, Alpha Lambda Delta Honor Society, Magna Cum Laude Degree.

Languages: German, Russian, French.

EMPLOYMENT:

1977-1984   United Distributers Corporation, Harris, Minn. 55941
UDC is a developer of distribution systems for Fortune 1000 companies. The product line includes order processing, inventory management, accounting, warehouse management, and multi-national applications implemented on DEC VAX/VMS and PDP-11/RSX-11M + systems. Positions held:

1983-1984 Contract Support Specialist

1981-1983 Manager, Customer Training

1979-1981 Junior Programmer

1977-1979 Computer Operator/Programming Aide

Accomplishments:

● Responsible for all phases of applications support for multi-national customer, including system quality control and applications deliveries.

● Prepared and performed initial software installation for UDC's first VAX customer in Munich, Germany.

● Provided on-site support for customers in the areas of database set up and operational procedures and problems.

● Managed all aspects of customer training, including defining customer training requirements, curriculum, instructor preparation, course costs and budget; wrote "Customer Training Guidelines" manual.

● Wrote and co-authored courses in the areas of System Operations, User Utilities, Database Maintenance, and System Management.

- Taught courses, including the above, at customer sites to audiences of up to twelve programmers, systems analysts, operators, and management personnel.

- Wrote programs using IDEAL including program specifications and programs for UDC's first conveyor/sortation system.

- Performed all aspects of computer operations.

PROFESSIONAL DEVELOPMENT:

1982   "Flawless Programming" workshop conducted by Roger White Associates.

1981   Digital Equipment Corporation Users Society (DECUS) Symposium in Houston, Texas

1978-1981   Digital Equipment Corporation, Educational Services. VAX/VMS Courses—System Management, Utilities and Commands, Concepts; RSX-11M + courses—Operator, Utilities; Introduction to Minicomputers.

1978   Minnesota Community College, Harris, Minn. Intensive COBOL; Introduction to Data Processing.

REFERENCES: On request.

ERNEST CAWLEY • 125 Forest Lane • Radnor, PA 19087 • (215) 293-0151

PROFESSIONAL OBJECTIVE:
Desire work on technical staff maintaining, developing or converting database systems, preferably on-line.

EDUCATION:
Wharton Graduate School, MBA 1967—Finance and Investments, Real Estate
University of Texas, BBA 1966—Finance and Banking

HARDWARE & SOFTWARE:
IBM 370/145, 158, 360/45, 55, 65; OS, VS1, HASP; IMS/DL1, DMS, ADABAS, COMPLETE, NATURAL; COBOL, FORTRAN, VSAM; WYLBUR, LIBRARIAN; CROSSTABS, UTILITY CODER, CITY PLANNER; OS/UTILITIES, OS/JCL

BUSINESS HIGHLIGHTS:

1976 to
Present

TREMONT INTERNATIONAL
Bryn Mawr, PA

Data Base Administrator

Responsibility for:
- Protection of IMS batch and ADABAS/COMPLETE databases, including physical and logical data integrity and security
- Hardware and software performance/response time evaluation and improvement on a D/B access basis using ADABAS and IMS Utilities
- Data Base design; both modification of existing IMS batch system and conversion to a new on-line ADABAS/COMPLETE system
- Education of programmers, analysts, and users in all aspects of IMS and ADABAS technology
- Maintain restart/recovery system for both databases
- Management of 3 assistant DBAs

Assistant DBA

- Responsibility for reviewing program design and IMS call structure for efficiency and conformation to installation standards
- VSAM, DBD, and PSB creation and maintenance as required
- Dump consultant and general problem solver for all IMS problems
- Taught classes to staff in DL/1 Concepts, Coding, Dump Reading; and ADABAS Dictionary, Coding, and Concepts

- Monitored VSAM space and ran reorganizations on 17 IMS production D/Bs, 7 logically connected

- Created and supported new IMS test D/B systems

- Wrote COBOL conversions from IMS D/Bs to ADABAS D/B

- Wrote ADAMINT macros; helped maintain NATURAL and Direct Call ADABAS programs, and COMPLETE screens

1970 to 1976	**HORNBLOWER & WEEKS, HEMPHILL NOYES & CO.** Bala Cynwyd, PA

Contractual Program Analyst

Handled short-term contractual assignments at various firms, primarily in CROSSTABS and UTILITY CODER, products of Cambridge Computer Associates

1967 to 1970	**ERIE TECHNICAL PRODUCTS** Erie, PA

Senior Programmer/Analyst

Maintained and modified large FORTRAN scheduling and routing softwear package. Considerable customer interaction. Attended IBM CICS Macro Level class preparatory to converting package to on-line

References on Request

PETER CHEUNG
32 Burton School Avenue
Westport, Ct 06880
(203) 226-7721
(203) 226-2124

EDUCATION: NEW YORK INSTITUTE OF CREDIT, New York, NY
1963-Business and Banking courses

MOBERLY JUNIOR COLLEGE, Moberly, MO
1956-1958-Business Administration

NEW YORK INSTITUTE OF TECHNOLOGY, New York, NY
Business courses (continuing professional education)

HARDWARE: IBM: S360/20-65, S370/168, 3033, 4341
DIGITAL: VAX 11/780
DATA GENERAL: C330, C350, M600
SIGMA: 7, 9 RCA: 70/35-45
GENERAL ELECTRIC C200, S400

SOFTWARE: IBM: OS/MVS, IMS/DC, TOS/SPF, DOS/VM/VSE, CICS/DL1, CMS,
Data Designer
DIGITAL: VAX 11/780, TOTAL, T ASK
DATA GENERAL: AOS, INFOS, INQUIRE

PROGRAMMING
LANGUAGES: Xerox's Certification Program for Applications Programmer PL/1, COBOL, IBM ASSEMBLER,
APL, RPG

BUSINESS
EXPERIENCE:
1982-Present NATIONAL BANK OF CONNECTICUT, Westport, CT

Manager Data Base Administration

Perform Database Administration functions and manage the Database group containing a
Database Software technician and the Program Librarian Function. The major area of support
includes a branch network of 89 offices, spanning 2 Data Centers. The system is
IBM/DOS/CICS/DL1 with 18 logically related Data Bases containing 2 billion bytes of data
over four major applications.

This year's activities involved establishing a Database environment and increasing the
performance of the existing Databases. Project Manager on the DBMS evaluation team, in
conjunction with an installation of a Product Delivery System. Responsibility for identifying,
implementing and managing the Data Security Function.

1977-1982 GNOSTIC MACHINES, INC., New York, NY

Data Base Administration

Provided project consulting support for online/interactive databases. This included database
design, data integrity, quality control, user interface, data dictionary definitions,
load/initialization logic, conversion specification, development of recovery/reorganization
methodology.

Project Leader, Machine Refurbishing Operations. This system contains subsystems for Inventory Control (6 separate plants, multiple storerooms, and shop floor), Order control (consolidation of external orders and trans-shipments between plants), Material Requirement Planning (consolidated requirements, usage history, and what-if reporting), Financial System (general ledger interface, transaction journaling, and financial reporting). Machine Tooling. This system controls tool and supply inventories, spanning over numerous tool rooms.

Database Analyst, Shop Floor Capacity Planning. This system supports fabrication shop with scheduling floor activities, tracking of machine and man hours, in an interactive mode.

Database Support, Computerized Process Sheets. Allows online Access/Maintenance of Xerox's assemblies process sheet, allowing use of common processes, phased implementation of new/revised processes, and line rebalances.

AMERICAN OPTICAL CO., Danbury, CT

1967-1977   Database Consultant

Provided project leadership of the Product Costing system/programming team. Team size ranged from 5 to 14 people; 18 integrated systems, over 500 programs and 3 different Databases.

Major Projects:

*Nonreplenishable Inventory Costing. Carried project from business proposal through implementation. Designed data structure, and middleware. This structure used IBM/ISAM/BDAM files allowing direct accessing of systems data thru 3 paths.

*Standard Cost System (Rewrite): This rewrite decreased run time of system from 40 hours to under 6 hours wall clock, and eliminated 3.6 million pages per year, providing a tremendous cost saving to the department.

*Interplant-Order Cost Detail: This system reports on direct material, direct labor, and overhead costs associated with international shipments of manufactured parts and assemblies to other Locations.

BANKERS TRUST CO., New York, NY.

1963-1967   Programmer Analyst

Provided project leadership for Product Costing System. Coordinated Standard Revision Cycle, provided expertise in system design, programming, and implementation of major system enhancements.

REFERENCES: On Request

Henry O'Connor • **145-96 Smart Street** • **Chicago, Illinois 60698**
(312) 598-9987—Home   (312) 598-4217—Work

EDUCATION   B.S., Mathematics, Virginia Union University—1974

COMPUTER   AMDAL V7
SYSTEMS   IBM 370/168
EXPERIENCE   IBM 370/155
                      DATAPOINT 6600 & DATAPOINT ARC

COMPUTER	COBOL	JCL	LIBRARIAN
LANGUAGE	PL/1	TSO	VSAM
CAPABILITY	DATABUS	HASP-ASP	CICS
	INTERACTIVE PL/1	OS/VS	SYSTEM 2000 DBMS
	FORTRAN	OS UTILITIES	

SPECIAL   Five years System 2000 DBMS (Data Base Management
QUALIFICATIONS   System) experience. Four years Project Management
                     experience. Five years COBOL and seven years PL/1 expe-
                     rience. Seven years TSO and interactive programming
                     experience. One year CICS experience.

SPECIFIC WORK/
TASK
EXPERIENCE
1976-Present   For the Illinois Environmental Management Agency

- Data Base Consultant and Project Manager for the Water Resource Division's Ground-Water Site Inventory System (GWSI). Duties included design of alternative system flow, development of extensive test plans, and supervision of project personnel.

- DBMS Subschema Programmer/Analyst on the GWSI project. For over three years, responsibilities included:

  —Performing systems analysis in determining use requirements for the GWSI System 200 data base.

  —Modification of the internal GWSI System 2000 data base structure.

  —Design, development, and initialization of test GWSI System 2000 data bases to be used in the development of GWSI system requirements and evaluation of procedural modifications.

  —Development of specifications for the design and development of DBMS interface software.

  —Conducting the GWSI/System 2000 user training courses.

- Data Base Analyst on the Water Resource Division's Ground Water Site Inventory project. Designed and developed System 2000 interface software which created and maintained the Water Levels data base. Software was developed using COBOL and PL/1 on an IBM 370/155 computer. Software utilized a subset of the GWSI data base and data independence properties of the System 2000 DBMS. Responsible for verifying the accuracy and completeness of application software by developing test data bases, test data, and a test plan. Tuned the software for correctness and efficiency by analyzing the test results. Completely documented the application software using structured documentation techniques including HIPO charts, narrative description, input/output lists, and module logic description (Chapin) charts.

- Programmer/Analyst on the PL/1 IEMA Mapping Project. Responsible for modifications to the Interface Program in which eleven new mapping options were added. The new software was tested, tuned, and implemented as outlined in the Project technical approach manual. A user's manual and complete documentation were submitted using structured techniques, HIPO charts, hierarchical tree charts, narrative description, input/output lists, and module logic description (Chapin) charts.

- Programmer/Analyst on a PL/1 interface and conversion system. Responsible for the design, development, and testing of this interface and conversion program. PL/1, structured programming techniques, development of test data, program testing, and a documentation manual of the application software were all included in the project.

1974-1976   Talco Insurance Company, Chicago, Illinois

The following major tasks were completed:

- Developed and implemented a computer reporting system that provides a cross check of the performance and accuracy of ISA, Talco's major insurance system being written in PL/1.

- Program conversion from autocoder to PL/1 which included analysis, coding, testing, enhancements, maintenance, and ISA compatibility checking.

- Served as MVS coordinator and senior PL/1 advisor. This involved coordinating Talco's conversion from SVS to MVS at programmer and programmer and program level and assisting with TSO, PL/1 and JCL problems.

PROFESSIONAL MEMBERSHIPS/ LICENSES   AIMS 2K (System 2000 user organization)

REFERENCES   Furnished upon request.

CHARLES A. SLABAUGH
930 Third Avenue, New York, New York 10022
(212) 758-9929
(212) 739-4455

JOB OBJECTIVE   Computer Quality Assurance Manager or Manager of Systems
                     Analysis/Programming

EDUCATION   University of Chicago, Chicago, Illinois   1979
                     Degree: BS—Physics
                             Minor—Mathematics

Technical Training:

                     Fundamentals of Data Communcations, ASI, St. Louis, Missouri—1983
                     Information Security Orientation Course, Defense Industrial Security Institute,
                         Richmond, Virginia—1983
                     Software Quality Assurance, Institute for Advanced Technology, Rockville,
                         Maryland—1982
                     Professional Military Management and Leadership, correspondence course—
                         1980-1982
                     Introduction to Honeywell 6000 System Software, COBOL Programming,
                         Entry Level GMAP Programming, 6 weeks—1981

                     Computer Languages:
                     COBOL, PL/I, RPG II, and INQUEST (Military Retrieval Language)

EXPERIENCE

September 1982   Data Automation Security Manager
        to   Military Strategic Command
    Present   West Point, New York

                     Responsible for managing information, personnel, and industrial security
                     programs relating to data automation of the Military Strategic Command. These
                     programs regulate 500 automation personnel and $20 million in classified
                     computer systems assets. Implement security education/training programs for
                     computer operators, programmers, and staff personnel. Determine personnel
                     eligibility for military security clearances and authorized access to classified
                     systems and controlled areas. Process visit requests for vendors and contractors.
                     Supervise 12 part-time assistants in administering the security program.

September 1982 to November 1979	Assistant Director of Computer Quality Assurance Program Military Strategic Command West Point, New York

Responsible for managing software quality assurance programs for large and medium-scale computer systems. Served as team leader in performing system management audits for a $9 million passenger and cargo processing system involving networked minicomputers at 20 sites worldwide. Reviewed, certified and published automated systems documentation, including user/operator manuals and technical design, development and test reports. Developed recommendations for improvements to software/documentation standards of the Military Strategic Command, and the Department of Defense.

Summer 1978	Student Programmer/Analyst Stewart Army Base, New York, New York

Completed the US Army Computer Systems Development Officer course. Developed an applications program to compute aircraft utilization rates for military flying operations management.

MISCELLANEOUS	Reserve Officer Training Corps, University of Chicago—1978-79
	Army Association member—1981
	Army Assistance Fund Drive, Project Manager—1981
	Officers Christian Fellowship member—1979 to present

REFERENCES:	ON REQUEST.

Lee D. Sofson
53 Fern Avenue
Greensboro, N.C. 28615

(714) 287-4908

OBJECTIVE
QUALITY ASSURANCE MANAGEMENT

EDUCATION

B.S.E.E. Tel Aviv Engineering College, I Div. 1965-1969

M.S.I.E. Arkansas State University, Russellville, Ark. 3.7/4.0 1970-1971

EMPLOYMENT

5/72-present Hydra Peripherals Inc., a subsidiary of National Advanced Systems, Greensboro, N.C.

11½ years of engineering and management experience in a leading high technology Magnetic Disk Drive manufacturing company in all phases of Quality Organization.

2/83-present

Position: Manager Quality Assurance—Subassemblies.

Basic Function: Manage a new department specifically created to improve the quality of subassemblies such as cables and harnesses, printed circuit assemblies, magnetic media disks, and power supplies procured within MPI and from outside vendors.

8/79-1/83

Position: Manager Quality Control.

Basic Function: Responsible for assuring that quality level of the operations meet or exceed the established goals at minimum cost through administration of effective defect prevention, detection, and corrective action systems during manufacturing process.

Scope:
*Coordinate resolution of product quality problems with feeder plants, design, manufacturing, and materials departments through closed loop corrective action systems.
*Provide quality departments input in pre-production phase of product; build and assure orderly transfer to production facility.
*Manage both inspection and quality engineering function to provide quick effective decisions on assembly/test problems to assure quality but minimize effect on schedule and cost.
*Develop and implement quality programs promoting statistical quality control and sampling techniques to effectively control cost and quality.

9/77-8/79

Position: Manager Vendor Quality Assurance (electrical).

Basic Function: Manage a group of engineers and coordinate their efforts to achieve optimum quality standards for all purchased electrical components.

Scope:
*Providing technical support to Purchasing, Material Control and Receiving Inspection
*Serve as primary vendor contact for communications.

5/73-9/77
Position: Vendor Quality Assurance Engineer.

Basic Function: Responsible for quality and reliability of specific components, vendor relations, Receiving Inspection support, and MRB.

Scope:
*Specific responsibilities included component design and specification review, writing inspection procedures, training inspectors, developing sample plans, work with vendors in trouble shooting, and assuring corrective action, evaluation, and disposition of rejected material and project cost estimation.
*Responsible for all semiconductors, specifying test requirements for various families of Integrated Circuits, coordinating test and failure analysis with centralized test facility.
*Responsible for all electromechanical and passive components from 5/72 to 5/75.

Accomplishments
*Instrumental in change of package requirements. Conversion to and qualification of plastic package for ICs. Resulted in savings of about $1,000,000/year.
*Achieved reduction in inspection work force through incorporation of statistical sampling techniques.
*Significantly improved the quality of subassemblies being received from all sources by establishing audit, reporting and corrective action programs.

9/71-5/72 Toshiba Products, Little Rock, Arkansas

Position: Supervisor, Incoming Quality Control.

Basic Function: Responsibilities included testing and evaluation of new radio, phonographs, and tape player chassis for home entertainment stereo components. Evaluation of defective components returned by customers during warranty period.

Paul R. Joseph
2803 Chesapeake St., NW
Washington, DC 20008
(202) 345-9876
(202) 433-3134

EDUCATION

1980-1983   Computer coursework: American University and Digital Equipment Corporation.

1978   Graduate School: University of Georgetown, Washington, DC; Statistics and research design.

1977   B.A.; Zoology, with coursework in FORTRAN programming and statistics. State University of New York, Albany, NY.

HARDWARE

Z80 microprocessor, Data General Nova 4, Nova 3, MAX-2, Honeywell 7712 ATM-Intel 8088 microprocessor, Incoterm 1525-Intel 8080, Incoterm 2040, Honeywell Level 6 minicomputer, *IBM 370, 360/40*, Honeywell 68/DPS (Multics), exposure to PDP-11/70.

SOFTWARE

Pascal, Assembly Language-Data General Nova, Intel 8086/88 and IBM 370, BASIC, FORTRAN, PD/FMS-File Management System, GCOS 6-Mod 200, Mod 400, (exposure to RSX-11M).

EXPERIENCE

SOFTWARE QUALITY ASSURANCE ENGINEER
Globe Data Inc., Washington, DC 1983 to present

Tested the Z80 micro based FOCUS real-time factory monitoring system.
Collected production statistics and examined production displays.
Designed and developed new tests and test procedures.

SOFTWARE QUALITY ASSURANCE TEST SPECIALIST
Apple Computer Products, Washington, DC 1982 to 1983

Tested the Apple Data Entry Machine's *Optical Character Recognition Software* for quality and accuracy.
Developed, verified and performed new test for the functionality of ADEM software (Data General Nova 3, 4, and MAX-2 processor).
Technical liaison between Systems, Marketing, and Customer Support Groups. Analyzed and prioritized software problems, identified by Customer Support Group.
Documented new releases of the ADEM's Optical Character Recognition software.

SENIOR PROGRAMMER
INTEL, Washington, DC 1981 to 1982

Designed, wrote and prioritized tests for software systems: WP 6 Office Automation Products, and 7712 Automatic Teller Machine (Intel 8088).
Assembled, linked and ran programs of the financial application software of the ATM utilizing the PD/FMS.
Involved in the implementation and the utilization of Diagnostic tests of hardware (Intel 8088 microprocessor and peripheral devices).

PROGRAMMER/RESEARCH COORDINATOR
Georgetown University, Washington, DC 1979-1981

Conducted data analysis of Astrophysics project, using the Honeywell 68/DPS-Multics operating system.
Supervised laboratory operations: trained lab technicians, performed research methods, collected data.

REFERENCES: On Request

Khanh Van Chen
488-1/2 State Street
San Francisco, California 94063
(415) 555-2345
(415) 555-1600

OBJECTIVE   Quality Assurance of systems software for the general marketplace.

EDUCATION   MASTER OF SCIENCE, Computer Science: 1983
San Francisco State University, California
Area of study: Systems Software
GPA: 5.6 (6.0 scale)

BACHELOR OF SCIENCE, Engineering: 1981
Merritt College, San Jose, California
Area of study: Systems Engineering
GPA: 3.5 (4.0 scale)

EXPERIENCE   STRATEGIC PLANNING, San Francisco, California

1983 to   Associate Programmer/Analyst. Strategic Planning develops systems
Present   software products for IBM mainframes. Primary responsibility was testing
new release of teleprocessing software product. Other duties included
assisting in the debugging process and preparation for product release.

(1977 to 1983)   Co-op Program (5 terms)
Assisted in system testing of DBMS software product. Duties included
development of test and diagnostic tools.

1982 to   NEW WORLD INVESTMENT MANAGEMENT, INC.,
1983   Oakland, California

Consulting/programming (part-time)
New World provides investment management services to pension and
profit-sharing funds. Installed a microprocessor-based UNIX system.
Converted existing software to work on UNIX system and use relational
DBMS package.

Consulting/programming (Jun 82 to Aug 82)
Developed an IBM PC-based computer system for portfolio management.

REFERENCES   Available upon request.

Edward Salson
144-30 Ford Brooks Road
Citadel, California 95610

Telephone: (916) 539-8486

EDUCATION: HUMBOLDT TECHNICAL COLLEGE, Humboldt, California
Degree: Pursuing Bachelor of Science (85% completed)
Major: Electronic Engineering

MERRITT COMMUNITY COLLEGE, Oakland, California
Degree: Associate of Science, 1979
Major: Electronic Computer Technology

EXPERIENCE: CHAPMAN SCIENTIFIC INSTRUMENTS, Citadel, California
January 1981   Product Support Engineer—Field & In-house
to Present

Responsible for: system design and development, installation and start-up, analysis of customer applications, and maintenance of CAD/CAM system, Graphics Systems, CNC automated drafting machines, photo-plotters, and all related peripherals.

Perform system hardware design development interfacing the CPU (M68000) to serial or parallel host computers, photo plotters, and peripheral devices. Test and analyze hardware architecture design concepts using: multi-bus computer oriented technology, multi-processor system, I/O function design, mainframe compatible system, slave minis, peripheral interfacing, computer commercial standards (RS 232, IEEE-488, ASC II). Write software test programs in Machine Code to exercise a certain hardware function.

Test & troubleshoot to component level the multi-processor-based digital & analogue systems—in-house and field (World-wide Travel). Product support engineering at pre-sales and post-sales levels from analyzing and prescribing customized system to training customers on system operation and maintenance.

HARDWARE: DEC PDP11 family, LSI-11, HP 2100 series, Zilog-Intel CPU's.
H.P.-WANG-Honeywell-Winchester-CDC Peripherals.

SOFTWARE: BASIC, FORTRAN, Assembler Languages.

June 1980   CALIFORNIA DATA CORPORATION, Oakland, Ca.
to   Electronic Technician
June 1981

Test, troubleshoot, and repair CDC's computer-based systems and peripherals. Diagnostically test to component level PDP-11, LA 30 and 34 Teletypes RH controlled bus TM03 and TMB 11 formatters and disc drives.

REFERENCES: Available upon request.

Lindsay Marie Wells
3546 Swarr Run Road
Lancaster, Pennsylvania 17603

(717) 955-2937

CAREER OBJECTIVE:	SENIOR MANUFACTURING ENGINEER/TEST ENGINEER
EDUCATION:	POLYTECHNIC OF GLASGOW, SCOTLAND B.S. PHYSICS AND ELECTRONICS, 1976

Studies included: electronics, circuit theory, atomic physics, laser, opto-electronics, computing (Fortran and assembly language), semiconductor theory. Completed course in introduction to work study from Production Engineering Research Association (PERA).

TECHNICAL
STRENGTHS: Experience in manufacturing, analog and digital design. Designing of: analog circuit, power circuit, logic, design of microprocessor-controlled hardware and firmware using TTL, MOS, CMOS, LSI, VLSI.

EXPERIENCE:
9/81 to   COMPUGRAPHIC, LANCASTER, PA.
Present   SENIOR ELECTRONIC PRODUCTION ENGINEER

Team leader, responsibility for introduction of new products to production, resolving manufacturing problems, participating in design reviews, redesigning product for cost improvement. Responsible for writing process specification test procedures; this includes evaluation of equipment needed for production and test interfacing with purchasing and vendors.

1/76 to
3/81   GRAHAM INDUSTRIES LTD., GLASGOW, SCOTLAND
                 DESIGN AND PRODUCTION ENGINEER

Famous company that specializes in electronics, microprocessor-based instruments, and production of various industrial instruments. Participated in production of writing layout, tooling fixture, procedure for test, description for kind of test required, and printed circuit board.

MEMBER: PHYSICS INSTITUTE

Paul R. Joseph
2803 Chesapeake St., NW
Washington, D.C. 20008
(202) 345-9876

OBJECTIVE: Computer networking, data communications, automation, computer systems management, and related positions.

EDUCATION: B.S.E.E. 1982
UNIVERSITY OF VIRGINIA
GPA: 4.66/5.00

SUMMARY: UNIX/C, DEC VAX-11/780 and PDP-11/70 UNIX, WE 3B 20S; FORTRAN, LCS, Wylbur, Insite, ICE; systems test engineering computer support; computer software and hardware configuration design; hardware interfaces design; high-speed link protocol analysis; systems administration (3B20S); plant-wide networking feasibility and technical requirements determination.

EXPERIENCE: MOTOROLA CORPORATION

8-82 to
Present

Systems Test Engineer

Performed computer support for systems test engineering at manufacturing plant. Designed software and hardware configuration of co-located computer systems. Designed all backup procedures; wrote system software; set up software packages; designed and implemented special hardware interfaces to processor driven test devices; performed engineering studies to determine feasibility of projects; performed protocol analysis for setting up high-speed links. Acted as liaison among management, system users, design organization, and support service in manufacturing environment. Served on a special task force to determine feasibility and technical requirements for a plant-wide networking project involving over 100 separate processors.

UNIVERSITY OF VIRGINIA Library System

1-80 to
12-81

Circulation Clerk

Utilized a computer data base management system, "LCS," which links over forty separate libraries. Instructed other employees on efficient use of the computer system.

Willing to
relocate

References
upon request

Randolph P. Simmons, 47 West 10th Street, Pasadena, Ca. 91106, (818) 372-4161

OBJECTIVE: Security Analyst

COMPUTERS   VAX-11/750, IBM 4341 & 370/168, PDP-11/70 & 34, DG M600 CDC 6600, MODCOMP IV, COMMODORE VIC-20

LANGUAGES   C, DEC & 6502-CHIP assembler, PASCAL, LISP, BASIC FORTRAN-77, RATFOR

EXPERIENCE   TRW, Pasadena, Ca. (Contract)
5/83-   Security Analyst-Programmer
Present

SECURITY ASSIGNMENTS: KVM, SURVEY, SBIR, PVS. Reviewed the Kernalized Virtual Machine study, which retrofits IBM's VM/370 operating system. (Study results allow much higher assurance of computer security at the cost of substantial degradation of machine performance.) Next assignment required a relational database system to analyze an Air Force wide survey of secure operating system requirements (including KVM). Tasks included database design, supervision of data entry operator, database verification, and presentation of statistical breakdowns for survey questions.

1/83-4/83   ALPHA DYNAMICS, Santa Monica, Ca. (Contract)
Programmer-Analyst

EXTENDED INVESTIGATION of FAULT-DETECTION for AN ELECTRIC POWER GRID USING MATRIX ALGEBRA. Devised statistical discriminant in Fortran to evaluate several hypotheses for faults. Implemented in Pascal the exhaustive revisions in mathematical argument for finding a measure of reliability for the observer's estimate of a fault. Also, VERIFICATION of C-5 SPECIFICATION of DESIGN TOOL for CONTROL OPTIMIZATION of ON-BOARD ATE UNITS.

12/81-1/83   DATA GAMES CORP., San Francisco, Ca.
(part-time)   Consultant

UTILITY DEVELOPMENT: GAME and EDUCATIONAL APPLICATIONS on A MICRO. Produced symbolic assembler with extended 6502 instructions, word-processor, and Lisp & Pilot interpreters. Modified Quicksort routine and simplified database retrieval system. Tested merging technique for interpretive Basic. Wrote several arcade-style games.

(Continued)

Randolph
Simmons

3/77-4/81   MEDICAL SYSTEMS, INC., Los Angeles, Ca.
             Senior Analyst

             PROJECT LEADER ON A MEDICAID CONTRACT. Designed the interviewee
             database. Also, produced exhaustive cross-tabulations and statistical presentations on
             selected demographic factors with SPSS. Directed a time-sharing vendor and
             keypunch group.

2/74-2/77   GENERAL GRAPHICS CORPORATION, Santa Monica, Ca.
             Graphics Programmer

             PRODUCED A SYSTEM FOR AUTOMATIC COMPUTER-CONTROLLED
             PATTERN GRADING AND DISPLAY. Used PDP-15 with PDP-11 as a peripheral
             processor, graphics terminal for interactive display, and marker-plotter controlled by
             HP-2100.

EDUCATION   B.S., 1974, Chemistry
             U. of California, Irvine
             Teacher's Certification in Mathematics and History, 1975
             M.S. Chemistry, UCLA, 1981
             Mathematics and Meteorology graduate courses at Cal Tech.
             Memberships in ACM and AMS

References upon request.

MARKETING AND SALES

MARIO PESIRI
859 Hobart Street
San Francisco, California 94110
(415) 875-9022

EDUCATION

1968   University of Wisconsin; B.A. in Economics

EXPERIENCE

Sept. 1980   SYSTEMS ARCHITECTS, INCORPORATED
to Present   San Francisco, CA
              Director of Sales

Responsible for managing the sales of Systems Architects'
Commercial Lines application products and application development software to the Property and Casualty insurance
industry throughout the United States. Duties include
managing the six-person sales force, product pricing and
promotion, demonstrations and presentations, and expense
control.

Nov. 1975   CASUALTY SOFTWARE AND SYSTEMS
to   Los Angeles, CA
Aug. 1980   Regional Account Manager

Responsible for the marketing of all of CSS's software
products and services to the insurance industry in the
West. CSS's products include insurance and investment
application software (OS and DOS), consulting, processing services, and satellite transmission systems. Duties
included revenue and expense control, efficient utilization of and direction of technical support from the corporate headquarters, development of the strategy to increase CSS's penetration into the insurance industry in
the West, and profitable execution of that strategy.
Sales Quota was achieved every year.

July 1968   HONEYWELL, Data Processing Division
to   San Francisco, CA
Nov. 1975   International Account Manager (Dec. 1973 to Nov. 1975)

Primarily responsible for managing the worldwide marketing of Honeywell data processing products to a large
multinational manufacturer headquartered in California.

Major activities included coordinating the marketing
efforts to the customer's 21 data centers throughout
the world, product and revenue forecasting, developing
and coordinating overall marketing strategy, approving
remote marketing proposals, obtaining customer corporate
acceptance of Honeywell recommendations, and marketing to

the large customer data center at the corporate headquarters. The position required both domestic and
international travel, the development of data processing plans to support the long-range business plans of
the customer, and the supervision of the systems engineers
and marketing representatives involved in this effort.

Advisory Manufacturing Industry Representative (Jan. 1970 to Dec. 1973)

Major activities focused on supporting Honeywell data
processing marketing efforts to manufacturing companies
in the western United States. Duties included: conducting both internal and customer seminars on the efficient
utilization of data processing equipment for manufacturing
applications, assisting in the development of customer proposals, conducting customer executive presentations, developing marketing strategies for particular applications
(i.e. Customer Order Servicing and Materials Requirements
Planning), writing application marketing guides for distribution to the sales force, and determining customer long-
range product requirements.

Systems Engineer (July 1968 to Jan. 1970)

Primarily responsible for providing technical sales
assistance to both marketing representatives and customers
for the successful sales and installation of Honeywell
products. Position involved the development of new systems,
proposal preparation, systems design, the programming of
new applications, and the installation planning for new
hardware and software.

References available upon request.

JOANNA CURTIS
29 East 12th Street
New York, New York 10003
212-669-7839

OBJECTIVE: Senior-level position utilizing marketing and technical
             expertise in marketing and/or planning and development
             of new products.

EDUCATION: Reed College, 1975 - B.S. Computer Science

ADDITIONAL
EDUCATION: University of San Jose, San Jose, California
             Graduate of Studies Program - Data Information Systems

             Wang Laboratories Education Center

             Management Development Seminar I/II
             VS Sales Training
             VS Analyst Training
             VS Customer Engineering Basic Class (operating system only)

EXPERIENCE: Digital Marketing, New York, N.Y.
1982 -   Office Automation Marketing Manager
Present
             Reporting to Vice-President of Sales, spearheaded the effort
             to off-load Corporate Marketing functions to the field; a
             move designed to establish closer communications between
             Marketing and Sales/Customers. Specific responsibilities
             include:

             *Analysis of market requirements and implementation of
              marketing programs within the seven states of the region.
             *Definition and creation of product strategies, product
              positioning and sales plans, new product introduction,
              and sales training.
             *Major/Commercial account product presentations and demon-
              strations, providing these accounts with future product
              directions, corporate overviews, and corporate direction.
             *Creation of the product marketing segment of the Office
              Automation division, which provides the primary interface
              between home office Market Planning and Development and
              the Area sales force for all product information and prod-
              uct enhancement criteria.
             *Design and implementation of the Western Area presentation
              and demonstration facility including all hardware/software,
              audio visual equipment, etc.

1980-1982   Sylvester Systems, New York, N.Y.
             Product Manager

             Provided business planning and life-cycle management for
             existing and future data management systems for all product
             lines. Defined product requirements, reviewed design and
             coordinated product development between R&D and Marketing
             organizations.

1979-1982   C.G.A. Software, New York, N.Y.
             Senior Marketing Specialist

             Responsible for providing product interface among field
             sales, internal development, and marketing organizations,
             with special emphasis on data management systems. Developed
             and implemented marketing programs and product seminars.
             Provided major account product presentations, performed
             market tracking, and analyzed products and market trends.

1978-1979   Beta Investment, Buffalo, N.Y.
             Data Base Administrator

             Within the Technical Support Group, performed sys-
             tems analysis for IDMS data base management system,
             IDD data dictionary, and CULPRIT query software sys-
             tem. Responsible for analysis, design, and implementation
             of the corporate data base system.
             Responsibilities included:

             - Physical data base design
             - Application system design review
             - Maintenance of program development standards
             - Implementation and evaluation planning for
               development systems

1976-1978   Travelers Insurance Co., New York, N.Y.
             Software Consultant

             Technical programming consultant performing customized
             design and implementation of vendor software packages
             for client companies. Responsibilities included:

             - Data Base Design - consultation with applica-
               tion development groups to ensure efficient
               use of the online data base.
             - Data Base Recovery - coordinated investigation
               and solution of "crisis" recovery situations.
             - Evaluation of DB performance and specified re-
               organization requirements.

1974-1976   Phoenix Mutual, New York, N.Y.
             Programmer/Senior Programmer

             Application development programmer with responsibilities
             for general ledger and accounting systems. Developed
             specifications and supervised the coding of financial
             management application.

References forwarded upon request.

THELMA L. CUMMINGS   175 West 73rd Street, #8G   New York, N.Y.   10025

WORK 212-960-2137   HOME 212-496-4142

EDUCATION

1974-1979   University of Vermont, Bachelor of Science. Major:
                   Business Administration

1979 to 1980   Boston University, Computer Science Studies
                   (BAL programming)

HARDWARE AND
SOFTWARE

                   IBM 3033, 3032, DECSystems-10, Commodore Micro,
                   6502, Apple II, VM/CMS, OS/MVS, TSO, TOPS-20,
                   FORTRAN, ANSI COBOL, BAL, 6502 Assembler, PASCAL,
                   FOCUS, CICS, IMS, ADABAS

EXPERIENCE

June 1981 to   APPLE CORPORATION
Present   White Plains, New York 10601

                   Product Manager (Software)

                   The product manager position involves all aspects
                   of software product management. The product, an
                   investment securities data base (SDB) system which
                   manages 50,000+ issues with daily pricing for 12
                   years, is licensed to major timesharing firms and
                   financial institutions. There are currently 10
                   installations generating over $1 million in annual
                   revenues.

                   Recently directed the development of a new IBM
                   version of the SDB product. Responsible for new
                   and enhanced user programs and development of VM
                   software tools for the user community. Designing
                   this software for a timesharing environment re-
                   quired exacting design and testing procedures.
                   Established a "trouble report" procedure for track-
                   ing and resolving problems. Responsible for main-
                   taining version consistency across different mach-
                   ines and clients.

                   Direct 4 technical (programmers) and 2 clerical
                   personnel in the development, implementation, main-
                   tenance, and customer support of these proprietary
                   products and data bases made available to the mar-
                   ketplace on IBM VM and MVS timesharing networks.
                   Products also include an APPLE II based product which
                   allows an investment analyst to automatically access
                   any of 7 different investment information network
                   services (Compuserve, etc.), download historical or

THELMA CUMMINGS (continued)

current pricing data on specified securities
issues to the micro file, and disconnect from
the network for off-line analysis of the information. Product is currently in Beta test.

Personally manage and participate in design
and programming of the investment analysis products using FORTRAN and COBOL on the IBM VM/CMS
and DECSystem-10 mainframes. Developed product
manuals and promotional material. Also acquired
familiarity with 6502 assembler and Commodore
microprocessors.

Nov. 1980 to   KESTON NATIONAL BANK
June 1981   Boston, MA 02110

                    Programmer Analyst

                    Performed both application subsystems development
                    as well as extensive OS JCL tuning to enhance per-
                    formance of production systems for this OS/MVS,
                    ANSI COBOL, IMS/DB shop. Developed and implemented
                    an extract system from General Ledger to provide a
                    more precise sales reporting system (OS JCL, COBOL).
                    Tuned the JCL to achieve a 40 percent improvement
                    in production run times, improved printing flexi-
                    bility, and system performance.

Feb. 1979 to   NATIONAL BANK OF BOSTON
Nov. 1980   Boston, MA 02521

                    Programmer/Analyst

                    Personally responsible for design and implementation
                    of a personal trust software package. Responsible
                    for design and programming of enhancements to exist-
                    ing master trust system.

                    Also worked with systems technical support staff
                    to supervise and implement a security system for
                    MVS called RACF, which monitors all open/close,
                    job initiation, and user logs. As disk space and
                    TSO coordinator, reduced run times from 10 hours to
                    6. Utilized BAL to develop screen formats under TSO
                    for use with COBOL application code.

1974 to 1979   GENERAL LUMBER AND MINERAL COMPANY
                    Montpelier, Vermont 23192

                    Salesperson

                    Worked as salesperson and then assistant manager
                    while studying for bachelor's degree.

MARVIN MILTON
24 Woodbine Drive
Cherry Hill, N.J. 08003
(609) 685-4212

EDUCATION:

BOSTON UNIVERSITY SCHOOL OF MANAGEMENT   Boston, MA
M.S. in Finance and Operations Management (1976)
    *Achieved a 4.8/5.0 cumulative average
    *Master's Thesis on Manufacturing and Field Service Issues
     was implemented at Data General Corporation

BATES COLLEGE   Lewiston, ME 04240
B.A. with Distinction in Business and Psychology (1973)
    Dean's List

OBJECTIVE: Marketing Director or Product Manager for Innovative
            Software or Hardware company.

EXPERIENCE:

1979-   Computer Horizons Corp., Trenton, N.J.
Present
            Strategic Planning Consultant

            Analyze products, markets, technology, and costs to develop
            effective market penetration strategies for CHC's clients.
            Clients represent the computer, petroleum, materials, and
            consumer goods industries. Work with clients from analysis
            through implementation of recommendations. Manage staff of
            15 business analysts. Have brought in new business.
            Accomplishments include:

                *Analyzed and implemented solutions for manufacturing
                 and engineering problems in a failing high technology
                 business.

                *Developed marketing plan and appropriate organizational
                 structure for a revolutionary micro-computer based
                 sensing device.

                *Analyzed and recommended capital investment and product
                 marketing strategies to combat cost problems and market
                 share erosion in a large consumer products company. Im-
                 plementation commenced after review by the Chairman.

                *Analyzed industries and companies to recommend appropriate
                 acquisitions for the re-structuring of a major corporation.

1976-   Turing Machines, Inc., Trenton, N.J.
1979
            Senior Marketing Specialist--Laboratory Data Products

            Hired to implement my Master's Thesis.

            Responsibilities included strategic and tactical issues,
            pricing, and business analysis for this large, technical
            marketing group. (Micros, mainframes, software). Reviewed
            all marketing and engineering development plans as a member
            of the LDP Management Committee.

        *Assisted in the re-organization of this product group
         to achieve a market orientation.

        *Implemented aspects of a strategic planning process.

        *Initiated several reporting systems to improve manage-
         ment control.

        *Developed analytical models to improve the quality of
         the management decision process.

        *Member of the Corporate Sub-committee on new product
         introductions.

Production/Inventory Control Supervisor

Line manager for all materials functions in a high-volume
manufacturing plant. Managed 35 people and cost centers.

        *Implemented automated manufacturing, planning, and
         control systems (MRP) which resulted in dramatic
         delivery performance improvements, lower inventories,
         and reduced write-offs.

Senior Manufacturing Planner

Analyzed and implemented solutions to manufacturing and
field service problems.

        *Construction of a focused manufacturing facility
         to support field service.

        *Centralization of Repair for the Corporation.

        *Improved stocking level model for inventories.

1973-   New Jersey National Bank, Newark, N.J.
1975

Section Head

Managed 3 departments (32 people) in the Securities Department.

        *Directed the planning and monitored the construction of
         an on-line securities accountability system. The system
         was the first of its kind.

        *Decreased manpower requirements while increasing control
         by redesigning the securities receiving function.

        *Planned, programmed, and implemented an automated coupon
         processing system.

References on Request.

Helen Roland
46 Robinwood Drive
Toledo, Ohio 43612

Home phone: 419-236-3715

OBJECTIVE

Position in Software Documentation/Marketing
Communications/Supervision.

EDUCATION

N.Y.U., New York, N.Y.
  M.S. Communications, 1971
Elizabeth Seton College, Yonkers, N.Y.
  B.A. English, 1963
University of Toledo, Ohio
  UNIX, Version III, "C"; 1981-82
Watson Laboratories, Cleveland, Ohio
  COBOL, Procedure Language, VS-100; 1980-81
Digital Equipment Corp., Cleveland, Ohio
  RSX-M and VAX Software, assembly
  language, MACRO-11, Utilities, PDP-11;
  1977-80

EXPERIENCE

1/83-Present

GENERAL ELECTRIC, Cleveland, Ohio
Advertising Manager (On-contract)
Responsibilities include space advertising,
direct mail, and technical documentation of
materials.

9/81-11/82

CUCUMBER COMPUTERS, Toledo, Ohio
Manager, Marketing Communications
Responsibilities included: press relations,
trade shows, documentation, public relations,
advertising, and promotions. Accomplishments
included: ground-breaking interviews with the
trade and popular press, hiring and managing
a six-member publications staff, writing and
placing technical articles and press releases,
managing a budget of $400,000. Cut $100,000
from the advertising budget and created an
open bidding system for publications. Also
began a telephone inquiry system, which reduced the cost of sales calls. Reported to
the Executive Vice-President.

1980-1981

IBM LABORATORIES, White Plains, N.Y.
Senior Writer for Telecommunications
Responsibilities included: Writing data sheets
and manuals, creating document plans, writing
product overviews for the field, directing
junior writers and editors, advising the Standards Committee. Accomplishments included: producing documents on the IBM 3270, 2741, and TTY

protocols, installing a review cycle for technical documentation. Created a set of product announcements for the Telex and TWX services. Developed platform skills for demonstrating Wang Office Systems.

1977-1980   N.C.R., White Plains, N.Y.
                 Software Technical Writer
                 Responsibilities included: documenting System II software system, planning a documentation set, answering inquiries from the field customers on the "hot-line," reporting to customers on new developments in software. Accomplishments included: writing chapters on system utilities, including the BAD (Bad Block Locater) and the PRESERVE utility for restoring files written to magnetic tape. Advised NCR's Educational Services on self-paced manuals. Wrote a financial systems guide for NCR 10s. Completed my computer education on System II's software.

1975-1977   N.Y. STATE COLLEGE FOR TEACHERS, Albany, N.Y.
                 Instructor of English
                 Taught Expository English and American Literature. Functioned as a program coordinator for ITV services, with special programs for foreign students and in British and American Literature.

References upon request.

                    ROBERT M. SMICK
        590 MORDECA STREET   SILVER SPRINGS, MD 20850
        Home: [301] 968-2404   Office: [202] 747-9201

OBJECTIVE: A position which would provide the opportunity
                to utilize a strong sales background within
                a UNIX environment.

EDUCATION: B.S. COMPUTER INFORMATION SYSTEMS
                Duke University 1977

EXPERIENCE: NEXUS SOFTWARE, INC. Silver Spring, MD
1983 to
Present   Position: Sales Representative
                Responsible for: Sale of C and UNIX based
                software development products. Target mar-
                kets include IBM 370 Mainframe Installations,
                as well as computer hardware manufacturers
                and value-added OEM accounts. Additionally
                responsible for evaluating and developing dis-
                tribution channels for the sale of company's
                software products to both the retail communi-
                ty and various system houses.

1982   BITS AND BYTES   Washington, DC
to
1983   Position: President
                Responsible for: Establishment of a software
                specialty retail distribution channel for
                IBM-PC and Apple Computer software. Specific
                duties included:

                  *Key man participation with venture
                   capital acquisition
                  *Development of short- and long-term
                   business plans
                  *Establishment of a retail sales or-
                   ganization
                  *Implementation of a comprehensive
                   facility to train customers on the
                   use of various business and system
                   software packages.

1979   COMPUTERWORLD RETAIL STORES   Philadelphia, PA
to
1982   Position: Vice President, Marketing
                Responsible for: Growth of a start-up per-
                sonal computer business to a position of
                prominence within the retail personal compu-
                ter industry. Responsible for the marketing

strategies and technical aspects, as
well as the overall company management.
Also implemented the advertising and
marketing strategies that resulted in
the growth from a single location to 3
outlets with gross sales in excess of
$2.8 million.

1977   DATA GENERAL CORPORATION   Pittsburgh, PA
to
1979   Position: Software Specialist
                Responsible for: Providing home office
                support for all Data General field support
                specialists. Products supported included
                COBOL and SORT. Interfaced with field sales
                organizations concerning all current market-
                ing issues.

                Also developed a time sharing accounting sys-
                tem. This system ran as a background task
                while "waking up" at intervals to accumulate
                and record system and user resource statistics.
                System also generated billing statements and
                management reports on a monthly basis. Also
                participated in the development of Data
                General's COBOL compiler for all versions of
                several operating systems.

REFERENCES: Available upon request

Pablo Gonzales
12 Prickly Pear Road
Santa Fe, NM 87524
(505) 239-8755

OBJECTIVE   Senior Sales or Marketing position with major Software
             Vendor.

EDUCATION   North Texas State University, B.A. Mathematics; 1967

EMPLOYMENT HISTORY

1981-1983   Software Systems of North America
             Santa Fe, NM

             As Account Manager, responsibilities included marketing
             DATABASE II and associated products in North Texas and
             Oklahoma and establishing a Dallas office. Attained quota
             of $1.1M, finishing 101% of quota for the year.

1973-1981   Forum Corporation
             Phoenix, AZ

             As Marketing Representative from February 1979-January 1980,
             responsibilities included marketing the entire product line,
             territory planning and management, and revenue forecasting
             and budget control. Ranked Number 2 in the U.S. at 216% of
             quota ($547,000 in booked business and 7 new systems in-
             stalled).

             Promoted to Senior Marketing Representative. Finished 9-
             month sales period of 1980 with $220,000 in business while
             developing a new territory.

             Was Marketing Representative of the Month in July and Sep-
             tember, 1979. Other positions held were Systems Programmer,
             Systems Engineer, Senior Systems Engineer, District Support
             Manager.

1971-1973   Information Leaders
             El Paso, TX

             As Systems Engineer in Life Insurance Industry Group, was
             responsible for entire Letters and Notices Systems for three
             life insurance accounts; for defining, implementing, and
             coding new letters for existing systems; for maintaining and
             improving existing systems; and for supporting application
             programmers.

1969-1971   <u>National Brands Corporation</u>
             El Paso, TX

             Among the responsibilities as a Systems Support/Programmer
             employee, was the responsibility for all DOS and Adminis-
             trative Terminal System implementation, Systems Generation,
             and maintenance.

1967-1969   <u>Xerox Corporation</u>
             Dallas, TX

             As Account Representative, installed OS version of OBS on
             the only OS/MVT/ASP triplex using a J65, I65, and J75;
             supported the CT systems programmers and teleprocessing
             group; and worked on sales presentations for hardware and
             software packages.

<u>HOBBIES</u>

Writing, music

<u>REFERENCES</u>

On Request

Willing to Relocate

ALBERTO ROSSI
One Top Stone Drive
Toledo, Ohio 43614
(419) 361-7444

EDUCATION

B.S. degree, Business Administration; Marketing Major, University of
California, Northridge - 1968

EXPERIENCE

HIGHLY VISIBLE SOFTWARE CO., Toledo, Ohio

12/82 to Present   National Account Manager

Sell a variety of software to run on UNIX-
based workstations, including Electronic Mail
and Word Processing packages. Received 4 top
sales awards; 1 of 2 salesmen in company to
receive sales award for exceeding $2M in sales.

CREATIVE SOFTWARE, Los Angeles, California

6/81 to 12/82   Regional Marketing Manager

Responsible for all sales, marketing, staffing,
and budgeting activity for four branch offices
located within southern California, Arizona, and
Colorado. Other activities included sales training, product positioning, product exposure, selling methodology, and sales manual development.

CSI/TEKNITRON, Greensboro, North Carolina

1971 to 1981   Major Account Manager

Marketing activity included direct sales to Fortune
1000 and California 100 companies. Succeeded in
selling and installing over 150 CSI Data Processing Systems, qualifying me for numerous "100% Clubs."
Involved in other projects such as competitive
analysis, sales training, and sales compensation.

DELTA/MICROFILM BUSINESS SYSTEMS, Durham, North Carolina

1968 to 1970   National Sales Manager

Established a national sales organization to market
computer output microfilm services. Responsible
for all direct sales activity, sales training, and
development of marketing policy.

PERSONAL

Willing to relocate

References available upon request

Reference Lists　9

Computer Industry Journals and Periodicals

The Bankers Magazine
Warren, Gorham & Lamont
210 South Street
Boston, MA 02111

Business Week, Industrial Edition
McGraw-Hill Building
1221 Avenue of the Americas
New York, NY 10020

Computer Magazine of the IEEE Computer Society
10662 Los Vaqueros Circle
Los Alamitos, CA 90720

Computer Opportunities
Datasearch, Inc.
4954 William Arnold
Memphis, TN 38117

Computerworld
375 Cochituate Road
Route 30
Framingham, MA 01701

Data Channels
Phillips Publishing
7315 Wisconsin Avenue
Bethesda, MD 20814

Datamation
Datamation Technical Publishing
875 Third Avenue
New York, NY 10022

EDP Analyzer
Canning Publications
925 Anza Avenue
Vista, CA 92083

EDP Training News
Carnegie Press
46 Hillcrest Road
Madison, NJ 07660

Financial Computer News
The Communications Exchange
1730 North Lynn Street
Suite 400
Arlington, VA 22209

Fortune
541 No. Fairbanks Court.
Chicago, IL 60611

Impact: Information Technology
Administrative Management Society
Maryland Road
Willow Grove, PA 19090

Information Systems News
CMP Publications Inc.
333 East Shore Road
Manhasset, NY 11030

Info Systems
Information Systems Pergamon Press, Ltd.
Maxwell House
Fairview Park
Elmsford, NY 10523

Legal Automation News
The Communications Exchange
1730 North Lynn Street
Suite 400
Arlington, VA 22209

Microcomputer News International
Elsevier Journal Information Center
52 Vanderbilt Avenue
New York, NY 10017

Mini/Micro Systems
Cahners Publishing Co.
221 Columbus Avenue
Boston, MA 02116

MIS Week
Fairchild Publications
Seven East 12th Street
New York, NY 10003

The Office
Office Publications
1200 Summer Street
Stamford, CT 06904

Recruiting Engineers and
    Computer Professionals
Cahners Publishing Co.
P.O. Box 716
Back Bay Annex
Boston, MA 02117

Small Business Computers
    Magazine
Ahl Computing, Inc.
P.O. Box 789-M
Morristown, NJ 07960

Small Business Computer
    News
Management Information
    Corp.
140 Barclay Ctr.
Cherry Hill, NJ 08034

Small Systems World
Hunter Publishing Co.
950 Lee Street
Des Plaines, IL 60016

Software News
Five Kane Industrial Drive
Hudson, MA 01749

Software Protection
Law & Technology Press
1112 Ocean Drive
Suite 201
Manhattan Beach, CA 90266

Systems & Software
Hayden Publishing Co., Inc.
50 Essex Street
Rochelle Park, NJ 07662

Telecommunications
Horizon House Publishers
610 Washington Street
Dedham, MA 02026

Today's Executive
Price Waterhouse & Co.
1251 Avenue of the Americas
New York, NY 10020

Training News
Warren/Weingarten, Inc.
176 Federal Street
Boston, MA 02110

Computer-Related Organizations

American Association for
    Artificial Intelligence
445 Burgess Drive
Menlo Park, CA 94025

American Association for
    Medical Systems and
    Informatics
Suite 402
East-West Highway
Bethesda, MD 20814

American Electronics
    Association
2680 Hanover
Palo Alto, CA 94304

American Federation of
    Information Processing
    Societies
1899 Preston White Drive
Reston, VA 22091

American Society for
    Information Science
1010 16th Street, N.W.
Washington, DC 20036

American Word Processing
    Association
Box 16267
Lansing, MI 48901

Associated Information
  Managers
1776 E. Jefferson Street
Suite 4705
Rockville, MD 20852

Association for
  Computational Linguistics
SRI International (EK 341)
Menlo Park, CA 94025

Association for Computing
  Machinery
11 West 42nd Street
New York, NY 10036

Association for Development
  of Computer Based
  Instruction Systems
Western Washington
  University
Miller Hall
Bellingham, WA 98225

Association for Educational
  Data Systems
1201 16th Street, NW
Washington, DC 20036

Association for Systems
  Management
2487 Bagley Road
Cleveland, OH 44138

Association for Women in
  Computing
407 Hillmoor Drive
Silver Spring, MD 20801

Association of Data
  Processing Service
  Organizations
1300 17th Street
Arlington, VA 22209

Association of Information
  Systems Processing
1015 North York Road
Willow Grove, PA 19090

Association of the Institute
  for Certification of
  Computer Professionals
35 East Wacker Drive
Chicago, IL 60601

Chinese Language Computer
  Society
Knowledge Systems Institute
Box 41
Glencoe, IL 60022

Computer Aided
  Manufacturing-Internal
611 Ryan Plaza Drive
Suite 1107
Arlington, TX 76011

Computer and Automated
  Systems Association of
  SME
Box 930
One SME Drive
Dearborn, MI 48121

Computer Law Association
6106 Lorcom Court
Springfield, VA 22152

Computer Society of the
  Institute of Electrical &
  Electronics Engineers
Suite 300
1109 Spring Street
Silver Spring, MD 20910

Data Processing Management
  Association
505 Busse Highway
Park Ridge, IL 60068

EDP Auditors Association
373 Schmale Road
Carol Stream, IL 60187

Independent Computer
  Consultants Association
Box 27412
St. Louis, MO 63141

Information Industry
  Association
Suite 316
Pennsylvania Avenue, S.E.
Washington, DC 20003

International
  Communications
  Association
Suite 828 LB-89
12750 Merit
Dallas, TX 75251

Internal Council for
    Computers in Education
1787 Agate Street
University of Oregon
Eugene, OR 97403

Inter-university Communications
    Council   Box 365
Rosedale Road
Princeton, NJ 08540

National Computer Graphics
    Association   Suite 601
8401 Arlington Blvd.
Fairfax, VA 22031

Numerical Control Society
111 E. Wacker Drive
Chicago, IL 60610

Office Technology Management
    Association   Suite 101
9401 West Beloit Road
Milwaukee, WI 53227

Society for Applied Learning
    Technology
50 Culpepper Street
Warrenton, VA 22186

Society for Computer
    Applications in
    Engineering, Planning and
    Architecture
358 Hungerford Drive
Rockville, MD 20850

Society for Computer
    Simulation
Box 2228
La Jolla, CA 92038

Society for Information
    Display
654 N. Sepulveda Boulevard
Los Angeles, CA 90049

Technical Manufacturers
    Association
200 Castlewood Drive
North Palm Beach, FL 33408

Urban and Regional
    Information Systems
    Association
Suite 300
1340 Old Chain Bridge Road
McLean, VA 22101

Computer Software Directories

Datapro Directory of Software
1805 Underwood Blvd.
Delran, NJ 08075

The Datapro Directory of
    Micro Computer Software
1805 Underwood Blvd.
Delran, NJ 08075

ICP Software Directory
International Computer
    Programming
9000 Keystone Crossing
P.O. Box 40946
Indianapolis, IND 46240

Data Sources
P.O. Box 5845
Cherry Hill, NJ 08034

PC Clearing House Software
    Directory
PC Clearing House Inc.
11781 Lee Jackson Highway
Fairfax, Virginia 22033

International Software
    Directory of Mini
    Computers
Imprint Software
1520 South College Ave.
Fort Collins, Colorado 80524

International Micro Software
    Directory of Mini
    Computers
Imprint Software
1520 South College Ave.
Fort Collins, Colorado 80524

The Computer World Buyers
    Guide
Computerworld
    Communications, Inc.
375 Cochituate Road
Box 880
Framingham, MA 01701